EXTENDED THEMATIC UNIT
A TRIP AROUND THE WORLD

Written by Barbara Schaff and Sue Roth

Teacher Created Materials, Inc.
6421 Industry Way
Westminster, CA 92683
www.teachercreated.com

©*1997 Teacher Created Materials, Inc.*
Reprinted, 2002

Made in U.S.A.

ISBN-1-55734-600-3

Edited by
Walter Kelly
Ina Massler Levin

Illustrated by
Cheryl Buhler
Blanca Apodaca La Bounty
Keith Vasconcelles

Table of Contents

Introduction

This book presents a unique approach to teaching. *A Trip Around the World* is based on the concept of a "living" curriculum. A "living" curriculum provides opportunities for students to experience subject matter rather than just read about it.

In this book you will find an integrated approach to social studies, language arts, science, math, life skills, and art. The use of integration allows a teacher to plan activities throughout the day that lead to a cohesive, in-depth study. Students practice and apply their skills in meaningful contexts. Consequently, they tend to learn and retain more. Both teachers and students are freed from a day that is broken into unrelated segments of isolated drill and practice.

Many of the suggested activities are designed to be done in groups. This provides students with chances to develop social skills, work cooperatively in groups, and practice good leader-follower group interaction.

The planned itinerary will take you on a trip that could last all year long. A variety of activities are provided for each country. If time is limited, it is not necessary to use every idea or every country. Shorter trips can be successful, too.

Using an Extended Thematic Unit

What Is Thematic Teaching?

Thematic teaching is a teaching method that allows the teacher to establish an overall interesting idea or a sequence of interesting ideas to which all of the skills and concepts required by the curriculum can be related. Learning experiences need to relate to each other and to the needs of the classroom. Thematic teaching allows for this.

The first step in thematic teaching is choosing a theme. This theme will be your focus in developing a unit for study to incorporate several curricular areas.

A central theme should have a broad area of focus. It should be adaptable to as many areas of study, concepts, and skills as possible. A good theme will not only allow flexibility in planning, but also help your students generate connections between subject areas. Bulletin boards and hands-on experiences related to the theme set the atmosphere for the classroom. Writing, research, cooperative-learning projects, and community involvement may all be a part of thematic learning.

Why an Extended Thematic Unit?

Themes can be as short as one day in length or last an entire school year. Although the duration of a theme is an individual choice, *A Trip Around the World* has been designed to take you through an entire school year. How you use the extended theme in this book will depend greatly on your comfort level with thematic teaching.

A Trip Around the World allows for in-depth study. Since the theme is carried on throughout the year, children are given an opportunity to become immersed in the topic. Activities of a wide variety are presented for you to meet your students' needs. In addition, bibliographies are provided that will allow you to choose the literature that will enrich your program. Using the passport on page 5 can serve as a reminder to you and your students as to what materials you covered. Although not every country in the world is visited, you may wish to extend your theme by letting the students do research on the countries that they were unable to visit.

A Trip Around the World gives you an opportunity to be involved with a theme that, through the year, will allow all the learning that takes place to interconnect, to relate to the needs and experiences of the child, and to provide some perspective of the world outside the classroom.

Planning Your Trip

Prepare for your visit to each country by gathering background information. Ask students to find the country on a world map (pages 8 and 9) or a globe. Then use the map of each country that is provided. Make an overhead transparency of the map, highlighting in color the places you will visit. Ask students to identify major cities and geographical features.

Ask students who have been to the different countries to tell about their experiences. Read books about the countries and watch travel videotapes. Bibliographies are provided for each country.

Facts About Each Country

To extend the study of a certain country or a certain subject (such as history), assign reports on the following topics:

- History
- Government
- Economy
- Agriculture
- Industry
- Education
- Holidays
- Foods
- Sports
- Art
- Music

Use these reports to add variety to your trip around the world. Concentrate on the foods of one country, on the arts of another country, etc.

Another option is to use these reports to show similarities among countries. Reports on industries, for example, will show that several countries share many of the same industries.

Vary the format of the reports so students can practice their skills in researching, writing, speaking, working individually, and working in groups.

Foreign Words and Phrases

A list of foreign words and phrases is included for each country. Practice saying the words. Have students use them in sentences and in stories.

Spelling Lists

Keep a running list of new words introduced during the study of a country. (Not all of these will be foreign words.) Use the list as a challenging spelling list.

Bulletin Boards

Design foreign language bulletin boards using cards of various sizes, shapes, and colors. Write an English word or phrase on one side and the corresponding word or phrase from a foreign language on the other.

Attach Velcro® to both sides of the cards and the bulletin board so the cards can be removed and turned over easily. Display the cards so that some English and some foreign language words are visible. Turn the cards over often.

Postcards and Journals

Encourage students to keep a record of their trip around the world by making a postcard or writing a journal entry at each place visited. Forms are provided on pages 6 and 7.

To help students get started, ask them to answer the following questions:

Whom did you see? To whom did you talk? About whom did you study?

What did you do? See? Hear? Eat? Learn?

When did you go? When did historical events occur?

Where did you go? Where did historical events occur? Where do current events happen? Where are important geographical sites located?

Why was this place included in the trip? Why would you want to return?

How does the geography of the region affect the people? How are holidays celebrated?

Another way to help students get started is to have them complete one or more of the following sentences:

The most beautiful thing I saw . . .

The most enjoyable thing I did . . .

The most interesting thing I learned . . .

The most surprising thing I found out . . .

Passport

As students travel throughout the world they will need a passport. A passport is a necessary travel document. It identifies the person whose name is on it as a citizen of the country that issued it. It also implies that the person carrying it will be given a safe passage through the country. Have students create a passport for themselves using the form and the cover below. They should fill out the information and either draw a picture or provide a photograph. As they travel from country to country they should get their visas. A visa is the endorsement placed on the passport that shows the passport has been checked. Use rubber stamps on passports as visa.

Name

Address

Age

Signature

Postcard Pattern

Travel Journal

My Visit To

_____

World

Map

Canada

1. **Map of Canada,** page 11

   Discuss the country's location, borders, geographical features, climate, and cities.

   Extending Activities:

   Assign group reports on the following topics:

   - Geographical diversity, ranging from its Arctic wastelands to the north, its fertile farmlands inland, to the tall mountains and lakes in the far west
   - Major citie—Toronto, Montreal, Vancouver, Edmonton, Calgary, Quebec City
   - Forestry

2. **Facts about Canada; Canadian Phrasing or Spelling,** page 12

   Have students color the flag. Assign reports as suggested on page 4.

   Canada has two official languages, English and French. Practice saying the words and phrases in both languages. Ask students to use them in sentences.

3. **Totem Poles,** page 13

   Extending Activities:

   - Read some legends about the thunderbird and raven often found at the top of totem poles.
   - Discuss how totem poles are created.
   - Find out about Thunderbird Park in Victoria, British Columbia.

4. **Salmon Fishing,** pages 15-16

   Extending Activities:

   - Discuss the life cycle of the salmon and draw a chart of it.
   - Find out which predators benefit from eating salmon.
   - Research to find nets that are safe for other sea animals. Discuss the types of nets used to catch the fish; include gill nets, seine nets, and trolling.

5. **Logging Industry**

   Extending Activities:

   - Research the logging industry, including how logs are cut and transported.
   - Read some legends about Paul Bunyan.

   - Find some of the various trees and research and illustrate them. Some trees to include are: spruce, ash, birch, hemlock, fir, beech, maple, elm, aspen, cedar, oak, Douglas fir.
   - Find out about sasquatch.
   - Research other legendary characters.

6. **Extinction Theories of Dinosaurs,** page 17

   Extending Activities:

   - Make a fossil out of clay.
   - Discuss the environment of the earth when dinosaurs lived.
   - Create a dinosaur mural.
   - Discuss the characteristics of some of the main dinosaurs.

7. **Ice Sculptures,** page 18

   Extending Activities:

   - Pretend to ride in an iceboat race across the St. Lawrence River.
   - Make an iceboat model.
   - Take a side trip to a glacier area; discuss how glaciers move and change the countryside.
   - Observe the aurora borealis. Draw a picture of it.

8. **Make a Canoe,** page 19

   Extending Activities:

   - Divide into groups. Research the Algonquins or Inuits.
   - Make model villages.

Bibliography

Nonfiction

BMcCall, Edith. *Gold Rush Adventure.* (Children's Press, 1962)

Fiction

Burnford, Sheila. *The Incredible Journey.* (Dell, 1985)

Nixon, Joan. *Fat Chance, Claude.* (Puffin, 1989)

Canada

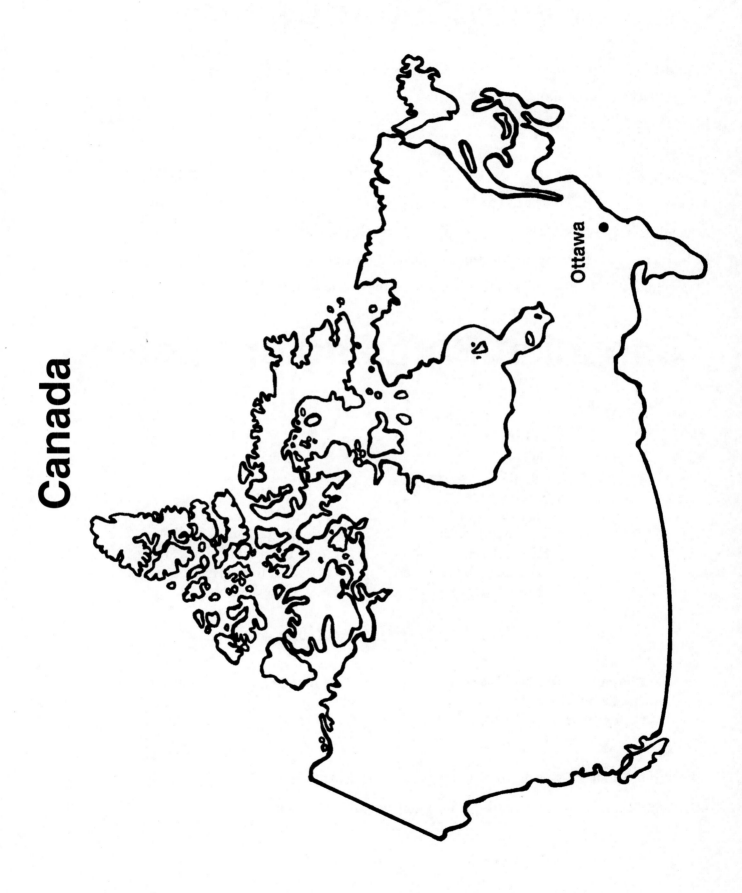

Ottawa •

Facts About Canada

Capital: Ottawa

Largest city: Toronto

Language: English, French

Currency: Dollar

Population: 29,700,000

Area: 3,849,674 sq. mi. (9,970,610 sq. km)

Agriculture: Livestock, milk, wheat, fruit, vegetables, feed crops

Industry: Forestry, motor vehicles, metals, minerals, fishing, food products

Flag colors: Left—red, Center—white with red maple leaf, Right—red

Canadian Phrasing or Spelling

English

centre	center
colour	color
jewellery	jewelry
theatre	theater
You're going, eh.	So you are going.
He's sick, eh.	I understand he is sick.
He's sick, eh?	Is it true he is sick?
How's it going, eh?	How are you?

French Expressions

Bonjour, mesdames et messiers.	Good morning, ladies and gentlemen.
Quelle heure est-il?	What time is it?
QuIest-ce qui est arrivV	What happened?

1. Write a brief story using some of the phrasing and spelling.

2. With another student, write a dialogue including this phrasing.

Totem Poles

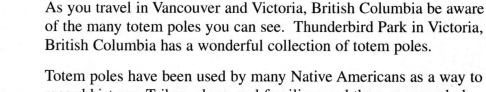

As you travel in Vancouver and Victoria, British Columbia be aware of the many totem poles you can see. Thunderbird Park in Victoria, British Columbia has a wonderful collection of totem poles.

Totem poles have been used by many Native Americans as a way to record history. Tribes, clans, and families used them as a symbol. A totem pole is a carving of animals, birds, fish, plants, or other natural objects that would represent a Native American tribe.

A family would place its totem pole in front of its home. At the top of the pole was the family totem or symbol. When a totem pole was erected there was a festival called a potlatch.

Make a totem pole that would represent your family. Think carefully what animals, fish, birds, plants, or other natural objects might represent you and your family. Then following the directions below create a totem pole.

Materials: clean, round ice cream cartons or small boxes, glue, paint, paintbrushes, tape, construction paper, paper plates, egg cartons, any materials to create a 3-dimensional effect

Directions: Using a paper and pencil, design a model of what you want to build. Choose a few different objects to represent your family. Once you have decided, stack the cartons or boxes one on top of another to desired height. Tape them together. Cover with construction paper. To create a 3-D effect, tape or glue on recycled materials such as paper cups, egg carton cups, or paper plates. Use acrylic or tempera paint to paint details. Display the totem poles in the classroom for all to see.

Butchart Gardens

One of the most beautiful flower gardens in the world is located in Victoria, British Columbia. This garden spreads out over many acres and features a Japanese garden, a rose garden, and a sunken garden.

In most of Canada spring-like weather does not arrive until after St. Patrick's Day on March 17th. However, in Victoria, spring arrives before then and Flower Count Week is celebrated. During this week people all over the city go out and actually count how many flowers and buds they see. Children are given an hour off from school to help count. There are special centers into which the numbers are called and a graph of how many flowers are counted is posted at Eaton Centre, a large shopping mall downtown.

Flowers play an important part in the decoration of Victoria, from the hanging pots of flowers on the streets to Butchart Gardens. Gardens take care and planning. Plan your own garden. After you have done your planning, "plant" your garden by drawing it onto a sheet of paper.

There are many things to take into consideration before planning your garden. Some of the things you need to consider include:

- What season of the year will you be planting your garden?
- What types of flowers do you want to grow?
- What colors will they be?
- How high will they grow?
- Can all the flowers be planted at the same time?
- What type of watering and feeding is necessary? Will they all require the same?
- Which flowers will you plant in the back? Which in front?
- Will you plant them all at the same time?
- What colors and types of flowers will you plant?

Use books about flowers, seed packets and information from nurseries to find out the answers to your questions.

After you have completed your research, draw your garden in bloom.

The Perilous Life Cycle of a Salmon

As you study the economy of Canada, you will soon discover that Canada's oldest industry, fishing, has been around since the 1500s. Making up nearly one percent of the gross domestic product, it is an industry that provides livelihood to almost 100,000 Canadians. Today you will find a thriving fishing industry on both coasts, and throughout the Great Lakes, but the majority of each year's catch comes from the country's western most province, British Columbia. Salmon, which is the industry's premier fish, makes up approximately two-thirds of the entire fish catch each year in British Columbia, making it worth almost 300 million dollars annually.

The life cycle of a **salmon** is unique and fraught with danger. The life cycle starts when the female salmon lays her **eggs** in the spawning grounds of her birth and the eggs are then fertilized by a dominant male, the adults shortly die after spawning. Three to four months later the eggs hatch into **alevins** (small fish, which feed from tiny sacs attached to their bellies). After several weeks as alevins, they become **fry** and begin their journey to the open ocean. As they head downstream, fry have to swim through dams, industrial pollution, irrigation canals, all the while eluding predators. If they make it through all of these obstacles, they will enter the ocean as **smolt**. Once in the ocean they will remain anywhere from six months to five years growing larger and changing to their final stage, an adult salmon. Finally, the adult salmon begins its long journey back to its spawning grounds. This time as the salmon head upstream they have to avoid commercial and sport fisherman, as well as the obstacles they passed through in their infancy. Once home, the cycle begins anew.

Directions: Cut out the boxes below. Paste them on page 16 in the proper order of their life cycle.

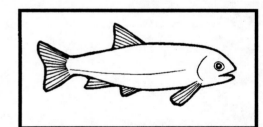

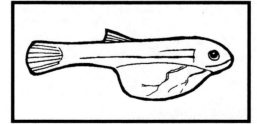

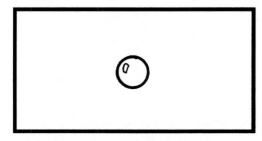
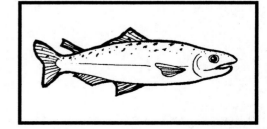

Life Cycle of a Salmon

Start

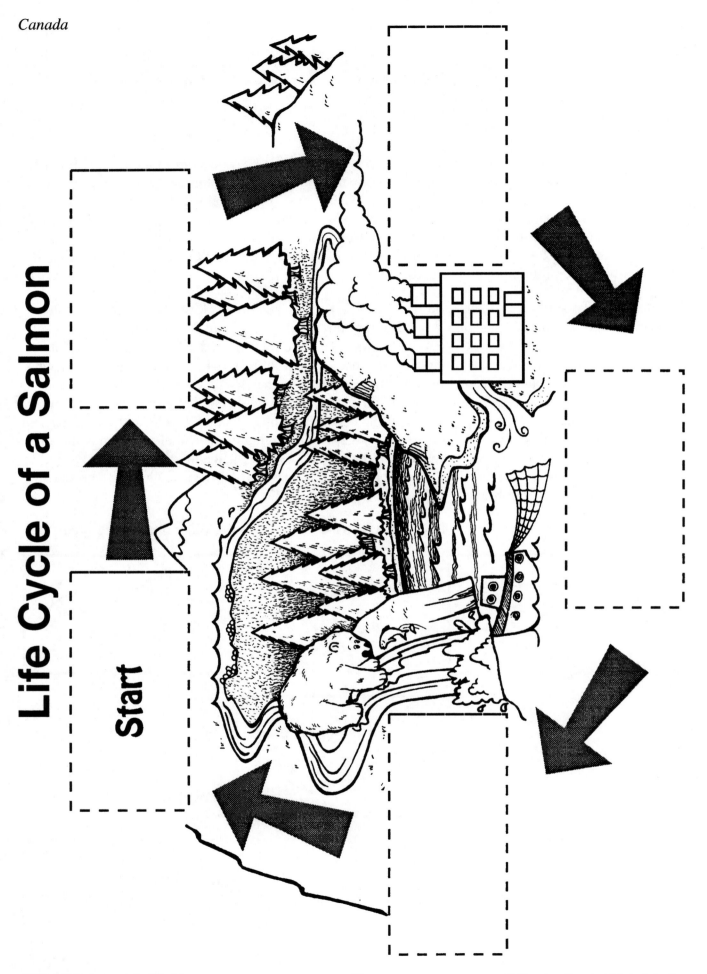

16

Extinction Theories of Dinosaurs

There are several places in Canada to see dinosaur bones. Many types of dinosaurs have been unearthed. The earliest known dinosaurs in Canada came from Nova Scotia's Late Triassic rocks beside the Bay of Fundy. The area was populated by prosauropods and theropods. More dinosaur remains have been found in western Canada. In the hills and valleys of Alberta's Red Deer River theropods and duck-billed dinosaur remains have been found. As a matter of fact, more than 500 skeletons of 50 dinosaur species including Late Cretaceous theropods, horned dinosaurs, hadrosaurs, and others have been found at Alberta's Dinosaur Provincial Park.

But why did the dinosaurs disappear? It is still a mystery.

Read some of the theories below. Which do you think is the real answer to the mysterious mass extinction of the dinosaurs? When you are through, write the cause-and-effect theory that you believe is the correct one. Justify your choice with at least three reasons.

Cause and Effect Theories of Extinction

Cause: A giant meteorite, 5 to 10 miles (8-16 km) wide and traveling at 50,000 miles per hour (85,000 kph), crashed into the earth.

Effect: A column of dust was thrown into the stratosphere blocking the sun and causing plants and other food sources to disappear.

Cause: A supernova (star) exploded very near the earth.

Effect: Extreme radiation covered the earth for a period of 10–20 years causing the plants and some animals to die.

Cause: Volcanic activity all over the earth temporarily destroyed the earth's ozone layer.

Effect: Too much ultraviolet radiation from the sun was allowed to reach the earth burning all exposed plant and animal life.

Cause: Volcanic activity on the sea floor forced the breakup to the continents and the shallow seas disappeared.

Effect: The land grew cold and animals without protective coverings, such as fur or feathers, could not survive.

My Opinion

Cause: _____

Effect: _____

Supporting Reasons: _____

_____

_____

Ice Sculptures

Visiting the city of Quebec in the winter, you may have the chance to attend the most famous Canadian midwinter festival, Quebec City's Carnival. This festival has been celebrated on and off since 1880. People come to participate in winter sports, watch canoe races in the icy St. Lawrence River, and view ice sculptures.

Try your hand at making an ice sculpture. Follow the directions below. Remember that unless it is very cold, your ice sculpture will melt. You may want to draw a picture or take a photograph to preserve it for yourself.

Activity

Materials: a freezer, water, several odd-shaped containers such as pie plates, rubber gloves, balloons, or plastic sacks, rubber bands, food coloring

Directions: Begin by deciding what colors you want your ice sculptures to be. Add food coloring to the water. Put water into containers using rubber bands to close off the plastic sacks or rubber gloves. Put them in a freezer and freeze overnight. (If the outdoor temperature is below freezing, you may place them outside.)

When they are completely frozen, remove them from their containers. Run a little warm water around the containers and then slip the pieces out. Stack the pieces in any way that you want in order to create an ice sculpture.

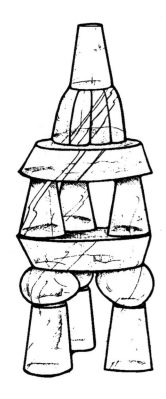

The Algonquins

Living in the Ottawa River region of Canada, which is now Ontario and Quebec, the Algonquin Indians lived in bands of 100 to 300 members, but hunted in groups of about 25. In the winter when they hunted for deer and moose, they traveled by toboggans and snowshoes. Canoes were used for transportation during spring, summer, and fall when they fished, gathered wild fruits, nuts, and roots. The Algonquins were known for their excellent skills in building and handling canoes.

Try your hand at making a small canoe out of paper, string, and glue. Follow the directions below to make a canoe.

Activity

Materials: brown or tan construction paper 12" x 18" (30 cm x 45 cm); crayons; scissors; white glue; string; stapler

Directions:

1. Fold the construction paper lengthwise. Draw a canoe pattern on it, making sure the fold will form the canoe bottom.

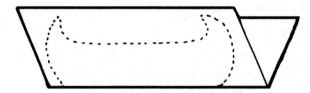

2. Cut out the pattern except on the folded edge.

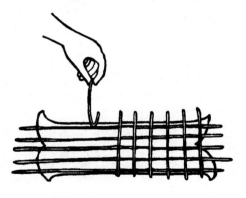

3. Open the canoe. Attach strips of string which have been dipped into thinned white glue, to the inside from end to end and side to side to create a frame-like effect.

4. When the glue dries, staple or glue the ends together.

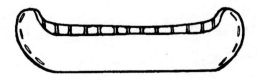

5. Add a paddle and paddler. Create a lake or stream in which to place the canoe.

Mexico

1. **Map of Mexico,** page 22

   Discuss the country's location, borders, geographical features, climate, and cities.

   Extending Activities:

   Assign group reports on the following topics:

   - Geographical diversity, ranging from deserts to tropical rain forests
   - Volcanoes
   - Earthquakes

2. **Facts about Mexico; Spanish Words and Phrases,** page 23

   Have students color the flag.

   Assign reports as suggested on page 4.

   Practice saying the Spanish words and phrases. Ask students to use them in sentences.

3. **Eating in Acapulco,** page 24

   Extending Activities:

   - Look at menus from local Mexican restaurants.
   - Eat Mexican foods prepared in local restaurants or the school cafeteria.
   - Prepare Mexican foods in class.

4. **Spending Pesos in Acapulco,** page 25

   The following answers are based on the typical exchange rate of 1 dollar = 3 pesos.

   1. 6 pesos
   2. 15 pesos
   3. 30 pesos
   4. 5 dollars and 0 cents
   5. 6 dollars and 66 cents
   6. 36 pesos
   7. $23.33
   8. 25 pesos; $8.33
   9. 24 pesos
   10. Answers will vary.
   11. Show pictures of Acapulco. Discuss why it is popular with tourists.

5. **Desert Plants and Animals in Baja California,** page 26

   Answer Key:

   Saguaro-H.

   Barrel-F.

   Prickly pear-C.

   Teddy Bear cholla-G.

   Scorpion-B.

   Gila monster-A.

   Desert tortoise-D.

   Road runner-E.

   Extending Activities:

   - Show pictures of the desert from books. Discuss adaptation of plants and animals to the desert.
   - Conduct an experiment. Compare a cactus and a small broadleaf plant. Observe and record their characteristics. Place in the sun and water when needed. Report results. Which needs more water?
   - Have each student choose one desert animal and find out more about it. What color is it? What does it eat? Is it dangerous?
   - Make a shadow box showing the plants and animals of the desert.

6. **Open-Air Markets in Taxco,** page 27

   Extending Activities:

   - Make silver and turquoise jewelry.

     Materials: aluminum pans and foil, clay, turquoise or blue paint.

     To make clay:

     Mix 2 cups flour, 1 cup salt, 1 tablespoon alum, and 2 tablespoons mineral oil.

     Add 2 cups boiling water. Mold the clay into jewelry pieces. Dry. Then paint.

   - Show pictures of Taxco's open-air markets, plaza, and cathedral. Notice the city's Spanish-style architecture. Describe the mining of silver.

     Discuss how a city's natural resources and climate affect industry, commerce, architecture, and lifestyle.

   - Read a story about a bullfight. Discuss customs and forms of entertainment.

Mexico *(cont.)*

7. **Ruins of the Maya in the Yucatan Peninsula,** page 28

   Extending Activities:

   Ask students to work in groups to complete one of the following projects.

   - Create a Mayan mural for the classroom.

   - Build a model of a Mayan pyramid and temple.

   - Make a Mayan calendar.

   - Write a story using symbols instead of words.

   - Show pictures of the rain forest and the Mayan ruins. Read about the Mayan civilization. Discuss what daily life might have been like for the Mayan people.

8. **A Fiesta in Mexico City,** page 29

   Extending Activities:

   - If you have old pillowcases, use them to make serapes.

   - Decorate the room with Mexican art, tissue paper flowers, and piñatas.

   - Teach students to do the Mexican hat dance and sing songs from Mexico. Or play Mariachi band music in the background.

   - Set up booths like those in the open-air markets of Mexico to display: Mexican foods, "silver" jewelry made by students, God's Eyes woven by students, God's Eyes woven by students, and post cards illustrated by students.

Bibliography

Non fiction

Coronado, Rosa. *Cooking The Mexican Way.* (Lerner Pub., 1992)

Smith, Eileen. *Mexico Giant of the South.* (Dillon Press, 1983)

Stein, R. *Mexico.* (Children's Press, 1984)

Fiction

Ets, Marie Hall. Nine Days to Christmas. (Puffin, 1991)

Desert Non fiction

George, Jean Craighead. *One Day in the Desert.* (Crowell, 1983)

Overbeck, Cynthia. *Cactus.* (Lerner, 1982)

Sabin, Louis. *Wonders of the Desert.* (Troll, 1982).

Desert Fiction

Baylor, Byrd. *The Desert is Theirs.* (Macmillan, 1987)

L'Engle, Madeleine. *Dance in the Desert.* (Farrar, Straus & Giroux, 1969)

Map of Mexico

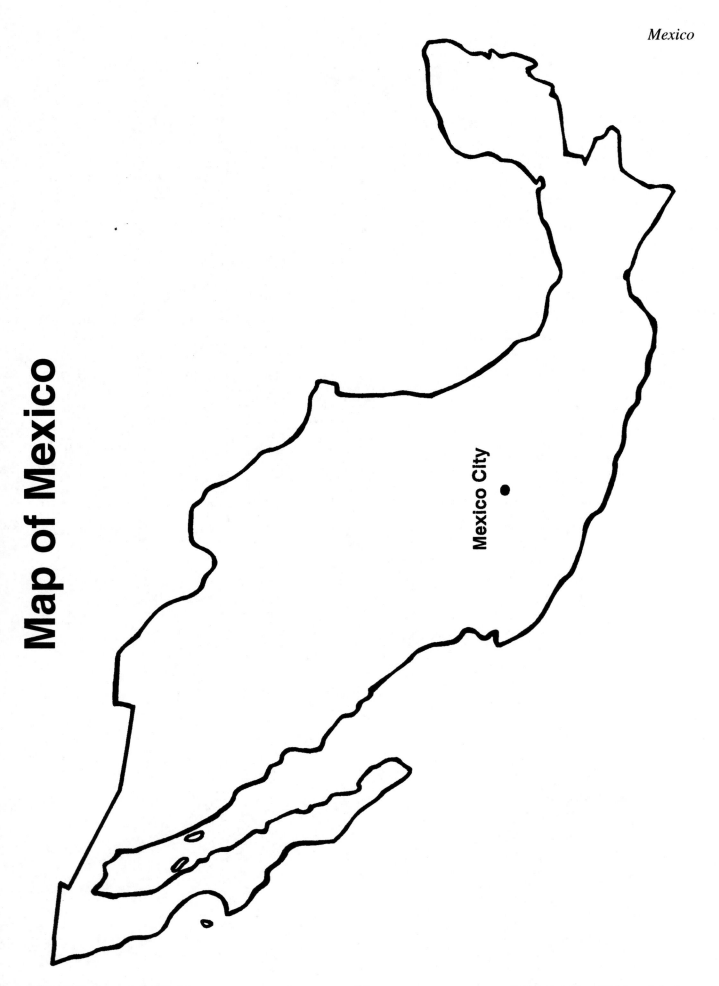

Mexico City •

Facts About Mexico

Capital: Mexico City

Largest city: Mexico City

Language: Spanish

Currency: Peso

Population: 94,800,000

Area: 756,066 sq. mi. (1,958,201 sq. km)

Agriculture: Corn, wheat, coffee, cotton, sugarcane, fruits, vegetables, tobacco, livestock

Industries: Oil, silver, gold, food processing, steel, chemicals, textiles, tourism, fishing

Flag colors: Left—green, Center—white, Right—red

Spanish Words and Phrases

Buenos días:	Good morning; good day; a common greeting
Buenas tardes:	Good afternoon or evening
Buenas noches:	Good night
Hasta la vista:	See you; so long
Hasta mañana:	See you tomorrow
Adiós:	Goodbye
Por favor:	Please
Gracias:	Thank you
La casa:	House
La mesa:	Table
La fiesta:	Festival; party
El sombrero:	Hat
La carne:	Meat
El pollo:	Chicken
El pescado:	Fish
El pan:	Bread
El agua:	Water

Add three words or phrases that you want to learn in Spanish:

_____

_____

_____

Eating in Acapulco

You have just arrived in Acapulco. You hurry to check in to your resort hotel. Then you go straight to the hotel's restaurant. You are hungry! What will you order for dinner?

Pescado a la Naranja
(fish in orange juice)

Arroz con Tornate
(Spanish rice with green bell)
peppers and tomatoes)

Ensalada de Ejotes
(green bean salad)

Tacos de Queso
(cheese, tomatoes, green chili peppers, onions, and sour cream wrapped in tortillas

Frijoles Refritos
(refried beans)

Tostadas de Pollo
(tortilla topped with strips of chicken, lettuce, cheese and avocado)

What is your choice? _____

Are you off to a healthy start? How does your choice match up with The Food Guide Pyramid below? List the food items in your dinner choice next to the food groups to which they belong.

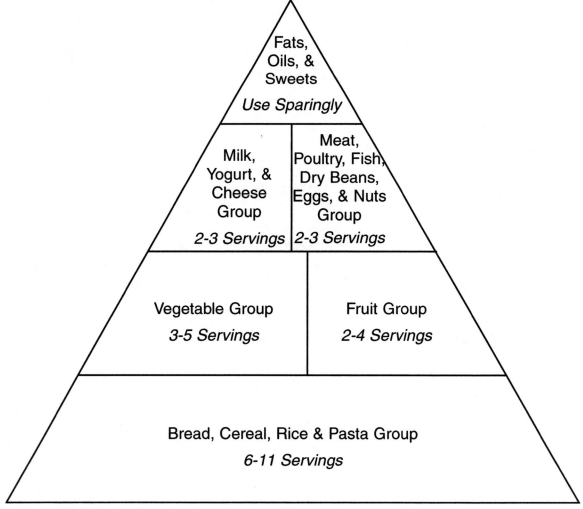

Fats, Oils, & Sweets
Use Sparingly

Milk, Yogurt, & Cheese Group
2-3 Servings

Meat, Poultry, Fish, Dry Beans, Eggs, & Nuts Group
2-3 Servings

Vegetable Group
3-5 Servings

Fruit Group
2-4 Servings

Bread, Cereal, Rice & Pasta Group
6-11 Servings

Spending Pesos in Acapulco

You are almost ready to stop. First, you need to exchange your United States dollars for Mexican pesos at a bank. You will find that 1 dollar equals 3 pesos. Then complete the following questions.

1. 2 dollars = _____ pesos.
2. 5 dollars = _____ pesos.
3. 10 dollars = _____ pesos.
4. 15 pesos = _____ dollars.
5. 20 pesos = _____ dollars and _____ cents.
6. You have 12 dollars. You go to a Mexican bank and exchange them for pesos. How many pesos do you get? _____
7. You see a blanket you want to buy. It is marked 70 pesos. How much does the blanket cost in dollars and cents? _____
8. You hear a shop owner and a customer discuss the price of a vase.

   Customer: "How much does the vase cost?"

   Shop owner: "100 pesos."

   Customer: "I'll give you 50 pesos for it."

   Shop owner: "I'll sell it to you 80 pesos."

   Customer: "I'll buy it for 75 pesos."

   Shop owner: "Sold!"

   What is the difference between the original price and the final price of the vase? How much did the customer save in dollars and cents? _____

9. You see a leather wallet that you would like to buy. You don't want to spend more than $8.00 for it. How much would you be willing to spend in pesos? _____

10. You have 50 pesos in your pocket. The following prices are listed outside a food market:

    Tacos con Carne (beef taco) . . . . 7 pesos

    Enchiladas de Pollo (chicken enchiladas) . . . . 8 pesos

    Bunuelos (fried sugar tortillas) . . . . 6 pesos

    Chocolate Mexicano (Mexican hot chocolate). . . . . 5 pesos

    Cafe (coffee) . . . . 3 pesos

    List three items you would buy: _____

    _____

    What would the total cost be? _____

    How many pesos would you have left? _____

    How much would you have left in dollars and cents? _____

Desert Plants and Animals in Baja California

Baja California is a desert. At first glance, the land may seem empty. But look closer and you will find many plants and animals.

Cactuses are most common in North America. They are well suited to dry regions. In most other plants, food for the plant is made in the leaves. In cactuses, it is made in the stems. The stems also hold water. After a rainstorm, a large cactus can take in as much as a ton of water. It swells and expands. Then it gradually shrinks as the stored water is used up.

In cactuses, leaves are reduced to spines. The spines help prevent water loss. They break up air currents, forming a thin layer of still air around the plant. Evaporation of water is slower in still air than in moving air.

Most cactus plants have sharp bristles and spines. These protect the cactuses from desert animals. Without the spines, the cactuses would be eaten.

Desert animals include many kinds of insects, spiders, reptiles, birds, and mammals. Most desert animals avoid the extreme mid-day heat of the sun. Some dig underground burrows. Others try to stay in shady areas.

Match the descriptions of desert plants and animals to the pictures.

_____ A saguaro cactus can grow to be 50 feet (15 in) tall. After a rainstorm, it can hold two hundred gallons of water by expanding like an accordion to store water in its cells.

_____ If the top of a barrel cactus is sliced off and the pulp inside is mashed, several quarts of juice can be obtained from the plant.

_____ The prickly pear produces a fruit that can be eaten.

_____ From far away, the teddy bear cholla looks like a cute, fuzzy teddy bear. But its sharp spines sting like needles.

_____ The scorpion is a small, but dangerous arachnid. Its poisonous sting can be deadly!

_____ The Gila monster is about one foot long. If left alone, it is slow and shy and will not bite. If bothered, it will bite, and its bite is poisonous.

_____ The desert tortoise digs burrows in the ground to stay cool. Its shell helps to reduce water loss and insulate the tortoise.

_____ The road runner is a bird that runs better than it flies. It uses its powerful legs and strong bill to fight and to get its food—insects and lizards.

Open-Air Markets in Taxco

Taxco is famous for its beautiful churches and its Spanish-style houses with red-tile roofs. It is also famous for its silver products. Talented silversmiths come to Taxco. Their shops are open to the street so people who walk by can watch them create jewelry, candlestick holders, drinking goblets, and other objects.

When you visit Taxco, be sure to visit the open-air markets. Watch the silversmiths at work. Look at the many other products for sale. Some of the items are woven by hand. You can learn to weave, too. Begin by weaving a God's Eye.

Activity

Materials: two sticks of equal length; yarn or cord

Directions: Make a knot joining the centers of the two sticks. Weave the yarn around the sticks as shown. Work from the inside out. Make a knot at the end and cut off the extra yarn. To design a pattern, change yarn colors.

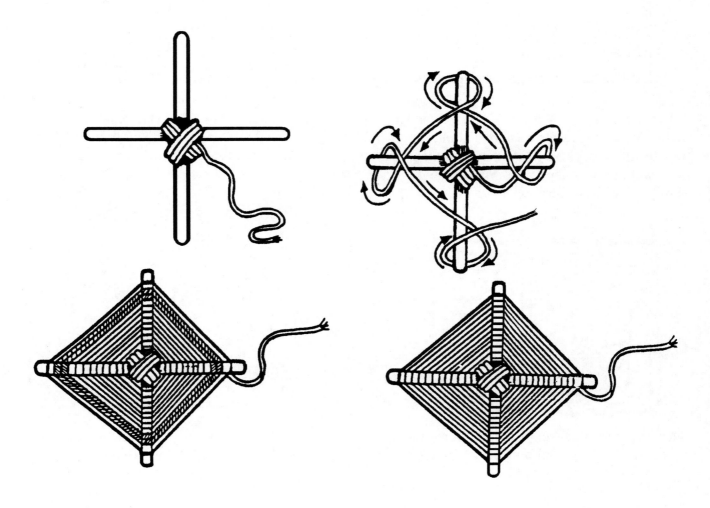

Ruins of the Maya in the Yucatan Peninsula

Bring your umbrella when you visit the Yucatan Peninsula! The southern part of it is covered in tropical rain forests. That's quite a change from the desert of Baja California! You will learn more about rain forests when you go to Brazil. Now you will do what most tourists do when they come to the Yucatan Peninsula. You will travel to the northern part of the peninsula. You will visit the ruins of the Maya (pronounced MAH-yuh) civilization. Find out more about this civilization. Begin by reading the information on this page. Follow up with some books in the bibliography.

The Maya civilization lasted from about A.D. 250 to 900. They made advances in both art and science.

They studied math and astronomy (the sun, moon, and stars). They developed a calendar with 365 days. A year was divided into 18 months of 20 days each. At the end of the year were 5 extra days. The Maya thought those 5 days were very unlucky.

They built tall pyramids of limestone. At the top of each pyramid was a temple.

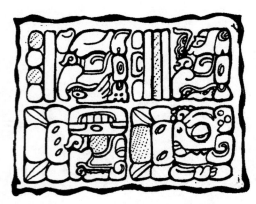

They developed a form of writing based on symbols. Each symbol represented an idea or a combination of sounds.

They painted brightly colored wall murals. These murals showed people either at festivals or in battle.

A Fiesta in Mexico City

Mexico City is your final stop in Mexico. It is the second largest city in the world. Only Shanghai, China has more people.

Mexico City is the capital of Mexico. It has a rich history. Mexico City is built on the ruins of an old Aztec city. The Aztec built their city in 1325. It was the capital of their empire. In 1521, Spanish invaders conquered the Aztec. Today, Aztec ruins and Spanish-style buildings can be seen throughout Mexico City.

Like all big cities, Mexico City has problems. Some, like earthquakes, are caused by nature. Earthquakes kill people and damage property. Other problems are pollution and poverty. These problems are caused by people. Somehow, people will have to find solutions for them.

On the positive side, Mexico City has more than 350 neighborhood districts. Each district has local fiestas or festivals.

To have a fiesta of your own, complete the following activities:

1. Make a sombrero from construction paper.

2. Make tissue paper flowers. Put a rubber band around the middle of a handful of tissues. Fluff out both ends so it looks like a flower. Wear them in your hair or use them to decorate the room.

3. Make piñatas. Later, take turns trying to open the piñata by hitting it with a stick while wearing a blindfold.

4. Perform a play based on your favorite part of Mexico.

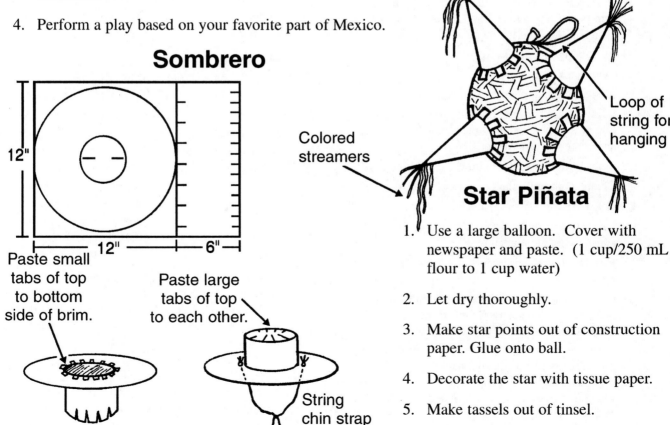

Sombrero

12"

12" — 6"

Paste small tabs of top to bottom side of brim.

Paste large tabs of top to each other.

String chin strap

Colored streamers

Loop of string for hanging

Star Piñata

1. Use a large balloon. Cover with newspaper and paste. (1 cup/250 mL flour to 1 cup water)

2. Let dry thoroughly.

3. Make star points out of construction paper. Glue onto ball.

4. Decorate the star with tissue paper.

5. Make tassels out of tinsel.

Brazil

1. **Map of Brazil,** page 32

   Discuss the country's location, borders, geographical features, climate, and cities.

   Extending Activities:

   Assign group reports on the following topics:

   - geographical diversity, ranging from grasslands to seacoast to tropical rain forests
   - Major cities—São Paulo, Rio de Janeiro, Brasilia
   - Agricultural strength—ranching, coffee plantations
   - Climate changes across the huge country

2. **Facts about Brazil; Portuguese Words and Phrases,** page 33

   Have students color the flag.

   Assign reports as suggested on page 4.

   Practice saying the Portuguese words and phrases. Ask students to use them in sentences.

   Extending Activities:

   - Notice similarities of many words to Spanish equivalents.
   - Research and report on Portuguese settlement in South America.
   - Research and report on the number of other European settlers in Brazil. (Have these other groups influenced the language?)

3. **About the Tropical Rainforest,** page 34

   Extending Activities:

   - Study the cacao plant and its products.
   - Study the rubber tree: present group reports on how it is grown and harvested, how it provides an economic resource for Brazil.
   - Study coffee bean agriculture.
   - Create a mural of plant resources.

4. **Plant Life in the Layers,** page 35

   - Discuss location near the equator and the constant high temperature.
   - Discuss almost-daily rain's effect on plant growth.
   - Create a large wall chart or mural containing as many specific plants (and their names) as you can find for each layer of the rainforest.
   - Research the reasons for the soil being thin and poor. Have students make a list of explanations. (Many people think because the vegetation is so lush, the soil must therefore be rich.)

5. **Rainforest Science,** page 35

   Extending Activities:

   - Visit a nursery that uses a greenhouse to force plant growth and raise tropical plants. Take pairs of thermometers for student groups to record temperatures inside the greenhouse and outside. Compare and report to the class.
   - Interview a nursery owner or manager or an employee. Ask for specific amounts and times for watering plants within the greenhouse. Compare this with the specific times and amount of water needed for his outside plants. Record data and place on a large chart in class. (Will more water be needed inside the greenhouse or outside? Why?)

6. **The Vanishing Rainforest,** page 36

   Answers to the problems:

Table 1	Table 2
20 blocks	1200 blocks/16 sq. mi./42 sq. km
30 blocks	1800 blocks/24 sq. mi./63 sq. km
40 blocks	2400 blocks/32 sq. mi./84 sq. km
50 blocks	3000 blocks/40 sq. mi./105 sq. km
60 blocks	3600 blocks/48 sq. mi./126 sq. km
70 blocks	7200 blocks/96 sq. mi./252 sq. km
80 blocks	12,000 blocks/192 sq. mi./467 sq. km
90 blocks	
100 blocks	

Table 3	Table 4
384 sq. mi./998 sq. km	2688 sq. mi./6988 sq. km
576 sq. mi./1497 sq. km	4032 sq. mi./10,482 sq. km
768 sq. mi./1996 sq. km	5376 sq. mi./13,976 sq. km
960 sq. mi./2495 sq. km	6720 sq. mi./17,470 sq. km
1152 sq. mi./2994 sq. km	13,440 sq. mi./34,940 sq. km
1344 sq. mi./3493 sq. km	67,200 sq. mi./174,700 sq. km
	69,888 sq. mi./181,688 sq. km
	Each year =70,000 sq. mi.
	rounded to nearest 10,000
	(180,000 sq. km)

   Extending Activities:

   - Discuss deforestation of the rainforest. Brainstorm possible effects and solutions. Make posters to inform others of the problem. Write letters to Brazilian government asking for information and suggestions for possible solutions.
   - Research effects of deforestation of the gradual disappearance of native tribes who made their homes in the rainforest. Develop a list of the names of the tribes still existing there.

Brazil *(cont.)*

7. **Writing Well about Brazil**, page 37

   Correct grouping of sentences into two paragraphs:

   First group

   1, 2, 4, 7, 9, 11, 13

   Second group

   3, 5, 6, 8, 10, 12, 14

   Extending Activities:

   • Research and write paragraphs about the cities of Sào Paulo, Rio de Janeiro, and Brasilia.

   • Research and write a paragraph about the Brazilian "gaucho" or cowboy.

8. **Terrarium Sentence Sequence,** page 38

   Correct order of sentence sequence:

   3, 5, 2, 8, 6, 9

   1 (Some students may elect to use this sentence last. If so, simply change all other sentences to the next lower number—2 becomes 1, 3 becomes 2, etc.)

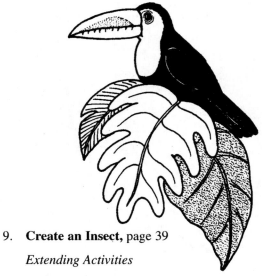

9. **Create an Insect,** page 39

   Extending Activities

   • Make transparent butterflies with newspaper, drawing paper, black felt markers, crayons, rags, and cooking oil. With black marker, draw butterfly on drawing paper. Color the picture with crayons. Place the colored drawing face down onto the newspaper. Use the rag to rub oil onto the entire back of the drawing paper. Hang the picture inside a window.

   • Make a spider web design. Draw a design on paper and cover with waxed paper. Dip yarn in thin glue solution (one part water to two parts glue). Place the yam over the design, overlap edges, and let dry.

• Develop a mural or collage of original or cut out pictures of animals of the Amazon. Include of the following:

agouti	ratel
anteater	sloth
armadillo	tapir
capybara	vampire bat
ocelot	parrot
coati	macaw
howler monkeys	anaconda
jaguar	cayman
manatee	bushmaster
spider monkey	fer de lance
opossum	piranha
paca	

Bibliography

Nonfiction

Cobb, Vicki. *This Place is Wet.* (Walker & Co., 1989)

Cowcher, Helen. *Rain Forests.* (Farrar, 1988)

Haverstock, Nathan A. (Ed.) *Brazil in Pictures.* (Lerner Publications, 1987)

Morrison, Marion. *Brazil.* (Silver Burdett Press, 1988)

Robb, Patricia. *We Live in Brazil.* (Watts, 1984)

Fiction

George, Jean Craighead. *One Day in the Tropical Rain Forest.* (Crowell, 1990)

Map of Brazil

Brasilia

Facts About Brazil

Capital:	Brasilia
Largest city:	São Paulo
Language:	Portuguese
Currency:	Cruzeiro
Population:	160,960,000
Area:	3,286,502 sq. mi. (8,511,999 sq. km)
Agriculture:	Bananas, livestock, coffee, corn, soybeans, cacao beans
Industry:	Autos, cement, metals, mining, chemicals, textiles
Flag colors:	Green with yellow diamond and a globe

Portuguese Words and Phrases

Bom dia	Good morning, good day
Boa noite	Good night
Atê logo *(informal)*	Goodbye
Adeus *(formal)*	Goodbye
Obrigado	Thank you
Como esta? (or Como vai?)	How are you?
Como e seu name?	What is your name?
Meu nome e . . .	My name is . . .
Sim	Yes
Não	No
Cidade	City
Roupa	Clothing
Casa	House
Dinheiro	Money
Escola	School
Rua	Street
Agua	Water
Fruta	Fruit
Olho	Eye
Cadeira	Chair
Carro, Automovel	Car

About the Tropical Rainforest

After reading the information about the rainforest, answer the questions.

Tropical rainforests are located in a narrow region near the equator in Africa, Asia, and Central and South America. Typically, these forests receive 15 to 30 feet (4 to 8 meters) of rain per year. They are home to 3000 kinds of trees, 1500 flowering plants, 125 different mammals, 400 kinds of birds, 100 types of reptiles, 60 kinds of amphibians, and countless insects.

Although rainforests comprise only 7% of the earth's surface, they play a vital role in the biosphere. They affect both the weather all over the world and the air that we breathe. They absorb harmful carbon dioxide and help supply the earth with oxygen. In addition, they are our most important source of raw materials for creating new medicines and a resource for timber, rubber, and nuts.

Unfortunately, 50% of the world's rainforests have already been destroyed. At this rate, it is predicted that by the year 2000, 80% of these forests may be gone. Until the problems of overpopulation and the demand for lumber are resolved, the destruction of the rain forests will continue.

Activities

1. **Knowledge**

   Where are the rainforests located? How much of the world's rainforest has already been destroyed? How much rain does the typical rainforest receive in one year?

2. **Comprehension**

   Explain the role that rainforests play in the biosphere. Name two problems that are contributing to the destruction of the rainforest.

3. **Application**

   You are a news reporter. Write a news story telling about how the rainforests affect our air and our weather.

4. **Analysis**

   List reasons why the rain forests should not be destroyed; list reasons why it is necessary to destroy these lands. Make a Venn diagram of your pros and cons.

5. **Synthesis**

   Pretend you are a bird, animal, or an insect that lives in the rainforest. Tell what it feels like to face the possible destruction of your home. Describe where you will go and how you will find food if your home is destroyed.

6. **Evaluation**

   If you were "King of the Rainforests," how would you solve the problems of overpopulation and the demand for lumber that are, in large part, responsible for the mass deforestation taking place in the rainforests?

Plant Life in the Layers

A rainforest is made up of layers. The **floor** is very dark and always wet. There is very little wind and very little change in temperature. The **understory** gets a little more sunlight and just a little less moisture. Wind and temperature changes are limited due to the thick canopy above. The **umbrella layer** (or canopy) is almost a continuous layer of green. When seen from the air, it looks like a large green blanket. There is sunlight above, but near darkness below. There is rain above, but a constant drip, drip, drip of moisture below. The few trees that break through the umbrella layer and escape into the sunlight form the **top layer**. These trees range from 120 to 150 feet (up to 64 meters) and have shallow root systems. They need to be propped up by an extensive above-ground system or buttress.

The soil of a rainforest is thin and poor. As leaves fall and decay, their nutrients are immediately needed for the dense vegetation. Roots absorb them and send them back up to feed the leaves and flowers. The recycling is fast. Fallen leaves in a rain forest do not have time to form deep soil as they do in the forests of North America. There is no winter rest period. The weather changes very little around the equator, and the plants are constantly working.

Floor: flowers, ferns, decaying material (very dark)

Understory: shrubs, small trees (filtered sunlight)

Umbrella or Canopy: medium sized trees which form a solid roof (lets little light through)

Top Layer (penthouse): 120-150 ft. (40 m) trees (full sun)

Activity

Materials: plant cutting such as creeping Charlie, spider plant, philodendron; glass of water; large, clear jar big enough to fit over the glass; two thermometers

Directions:

1. Put the cutting in the glass of water and allow it to root. Make a chart of the daily growth of the root system. (This part of the activity takes about a week.)
2. Put an inverted jar over the cutting in the glass of water. Place in the sunlight.
3. Put a thermometer inside the jar to monitor the temperature. Put another thermometer beside the jar to monitor the difference between the outside temperature and the temperature inside the jar. Wait one hour and check results.

Answer the following questions:

1. What happens to the temperature inside the jar? Why do you think that is?
2. What happens to the water inside the jar? Why do you think that happens?

HINT: The jar works the same way as the umbrella layer in a rainforest. It traps the moisture and the heat. (After the experiment, plant your cutting in a moist, shaded area and watch it grow or keep it as a classroom plant.)

The Vanishing Rainforest

Each minute of each day, an area of rainforest the size of ten city blocks vanishes from Earth, according to some calculations. Complete the following tables to find out how much rainforest disappears each year. (Note: You may use a calculator. These measurements are approximate and rounded. Do not write in the gray areas.)

Table 1

1 minute	10 blocks
2 minutes	20 blocks
3 minutes	
4 minutes	
5 minutes	
6 minutes	
7 minutes	
8 minutes	
9 minutes	
10 minutes	
60 minutes	

Table 2

1 hour	600 blocks	8 sq. mi. (21 sq. km)
2 hours		
3 hours		
4 hours		
5 hours		
6 hours		
12 hours		
24 hours		

Table 3

1 day	192 sq. miles (499 sq. km)
2 days	
3 days	
4 days	
5 days	
6 days	
7 days	

Table 4

1 week	1,344 sq. miles (3,494 sq. km)
2 weeks	
3 weeks	
4 weeks	
5 weeks	
10 weeks	
50 weeks	
52 weeks	

About how much rainforest vanishes each year? _____

(Round to the nearest 10,000)

36

Writing Well About Brazil

Good writers want to help readers understand and remember what they read. To do this, they "bundle" their sentences into groups of separate topics. These bundles or groups are called "paragraphs." In other words, a paragraph is no more than a bundle of sentences, all of them addressing one topic. You might write a story about Brazil, for example. One paragraph might be about the city of São Paulo, or Rio de Janeiro, or Brasilia. Another might discuss the fanning in the Matto Grosso. The sentences below are all about Brazil, but if you look closely, you will see that the writer really could have helped the reader by bundling his sentences into two separate paragraphs. Can you separate these sentences into two groups so we all can understand and remember the information better? Write your two paragraphs on the lines below.

(1) In Brazil, tropical forests surround the Amazon River near the equator. (2) These tropical forests are called "rainforests" because they receive more than 100 inches (254 cm) of rain per year. (3) The Amazon Region has a great variety of animals. (4) The forests have fairly clear ground areas because the tall trees shut out the light to the floor of the forest. (5) More than 1500 kinds of birds live in the forests. (6) Toucans, parrots, parakeets, and other rainbow-hued birds sing and squawk from the towering branches. (7) The floor is very dark and always wet. (8) Many kinds of screeching, howling monkeys leap through the trees, supplementing the bird calls. (9) There is rain above but a constant drip, drip, drip of moisture below. (10) Ants, beetles, butterflies, and other insects live throughout the region. (11) The soil is thin and poor. (12) Huge boa constrictors and anacondas up to 30 feet long (9 meters) silently glide along the branches and by the rivers. (13) These forests are located in climatic areas where hot temperatures are nearly year-round, so the trees and plants that grow there are green and lush all year. (14) Other Amazon animals include anteaters, sloths, tapirs, powerful jaguars, caymans, and capybaras—the world's largest rodents.

Terrarium Sentence Sequence

Good writers not only want to help the reader understand and remember, they also want to help the reader avoid becoming confused. One way to do this is to write their sentences in a correct and helpful order. This is called using proper "sequence." See if you can rearrange the following sentences in a sequence that makes a helpful paragraph for the reader. (Notice that this will also help clarify your own thinking.)

Activity

On the lines below, rewrite the following sentences in proper sequence. Once you have the directions in the correct order, you may wish to follow them and build your own rainforest terrarium.

How to Build a Rainforest Terrarium

1. Layer the gravel and then the charcoal on the bottom of the tank.

2. Cover the stones with about an inch of compost.

3. First, you will need a large fish tank, gravel, charcoal, compost, small stones, moss, bromeliads, small ferns, and water.

4. Cover your terrarium with a glass top or tight-fitting sheet of plastic wrap.

5. Dampen the compost with water and plant the ferns, moss, and bromeliads.

6. Keep the terrarium in a warm spot out of direct sunlight.

7. Building a rainforest terrarium can be easy and instructive if you follow directions carefully.

8. Spread the small stones over the gravel, creating small hills and valleys.

9. Allow plenty of space between the plants.

10. After a few months, you may have to add a little water.

1. _____

2. _____

3. _____

4. _____

5. _____

6. _____

7. _____

8. _____

9. _____

10. _____

Create an Insect

The jungles and rainforests of the earth contain millions of types of insects. Many are undiscovered and unclassified. Use the following characteristics and your imagination to create an insect. Name it after the famous scientist who is first bringing it to the world's attention — you!

- All insects have three body parts — head, thorax, and abdomen.
- All insects have six jointed legs.
- The head has eyes, antennae, and a mouth that sucks or chews.
- The thorax has six legs (three on each side) and usually four wings. Some wings help an insect fly, and some wings protect. Wings are always symmetrical — one side is the same size, shape, and color as the other.
- The abdomen has ten or eleven segments. You can usually see five to eight of them.

Activity

Use the patterns below (or make some of your own) to create an insect. Trace on construction paper, cut out, and glue together. Be sure your insect has three body parts and six jointed legs. Add color and details with crayon, markers, tissue paper, etc.

Australia

1. **Map of Australia,** page 41

   Discuss the country's location, borders, geographical features, climate, and cities.

   Extending Activities:

   Assign group reports on the following topics:
   - Geographical diversity, ranging from deserts to tropical rain forests to Australian Alps.
   - Population density, early European settlement, exploration

2. **Facts About Australia; Australian Slang Words and Phrases,** page 42

   Have students color flag.
   Assign reports as suggested on page 4.
   Practice using Australian slang.

3. **Sydney Opera House,** page 43

   Discuss Sydney Opera House location, structure, architecture, size.
   Discuss symphony, opera, ballet, classical composers.

   Extending Activities:
   - Listen to classical music tapes.
   - Attend local concert.

4. **Visit a Game Preserve,** page 44
   - Discuss mammals and marsupials.
   - Identify marsupials living outside of Australia and reasons for so many marsupials existing in Australia.

   Extending Activities:
   - Visit local zoo or animal park.
   - Show films or videos of Australian animals.

5. **Camping Out in the Bush,** pages 45-46
   - Discuss and compare lists and costs of supplies. Are all items practical? Was anything overlooked?
   - Discuss constellations in the hemispheres.
   - Identify Southern Cross, Dippers, and North Star.

   Extending Activities:
   - Visit a planetarium.
   - Build a star-viewing box telescope.
   - Observe the moon with binoculars.
   - Read stories (myths) of the origin of constellations.

6. **Australian Aborigines,** page 46

   Extending Activities:
   - Discuss stories read orally to class.
   - Read student-created origin stories.
   - Show pictures of Aborigine cave paintings.
   - Research "walkabout" customs of Aborigines.

7. **The Australian Outback,** page 47

   Extending Activities:
   - Orally compare class emergency lists and supplies.
   - Research Australian sheep dogs — breeds, colors, sizes, shapes, characteristics, abilities, lifespan.
   - Bring pictures of sheep and cattle dogs of Australia.

8. **The Great Barrier Reef,** page 48

   Extending Activities:
   - Visit a local aquarium.
   - View videos or films of coral reefs.
   - Research sharks—types, favorite food, size, range
   - Have students bring shells, sea urchin and starfish skeletons, coral, etc., for classroom display.
   - Create a wall coral reef mural with wrapping paper as background. Cut out pictures of various types of coral and sea creatures. Label.

Bibliography

Fiction

Baker, Jeannie. *Where the Forest Meets the Sea.* (Greenwillow, 1988)

Base, Graeme. *My Grandma Lived in Gooligulch.* (Australian Book Service, 1988)

Cole, Joanna (selected by). *Best Loved Folktales of the World.* (Doubleday, 1982)

Map of Australia

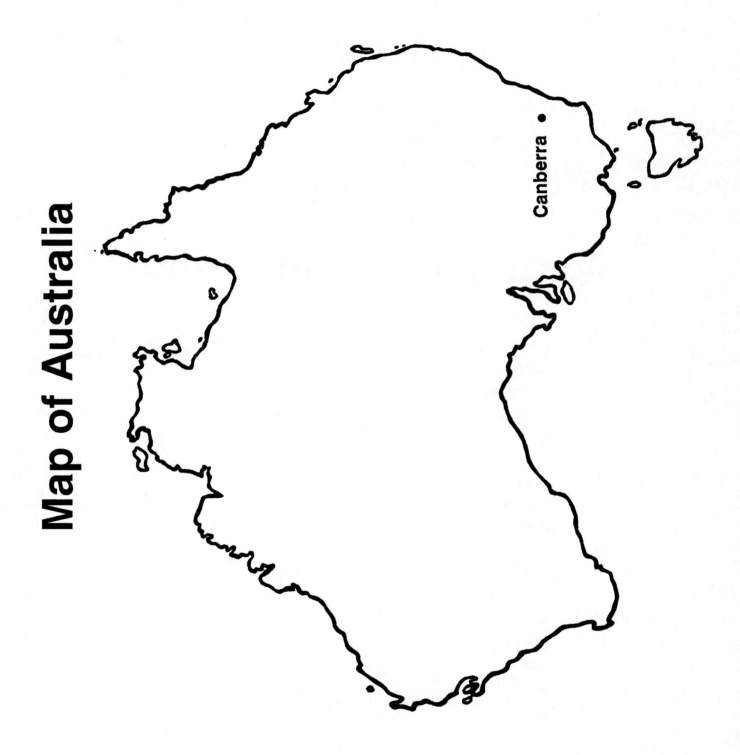

Canberra

Facts About Australia

Capital:	Canberra
Largest city:	Sydney
Language:	English
Currency:	Dollar
Population:	18,758,000
Area:	2,978,147 sq. mi. (7,713,364 sq. km)
Agriculture:	Apples, barley, livestock, milk, grapes
Industries:	Forestry, automobiles, textiles, iron, steel, coal
Flag colors:	Navy blue with six white stars

Australian Slang Terms

Roo	Kangaroo
Bonzer	Terrific
Walloper	Policeman
Bushranger	Outlaw
Barby	Barbecue
Good on ya!	Good for you!
Joey	Baby kangaroo
Footie	Football
Mossies	Mosquitoes
Bloke	Man, fellow, chap
Walkabout	To wander
Petrol	Gasoline
Takeaway	Fast food shop
Lolly shop	Candy store
Squatter	Ranch owner
Mate	Friend
Tucker	Food
Bush	Countryside

1. Create ten sentences using at least one of the above terms in each.

2. Write a brief story containing several of the above terms.

3. With another student, write a dialogue using the above terms.

Sydney Opera House

As you arrive in Sydney, the largest city of Australia, you will spy one of the world's most distinctive buildings—the Sydney Opera House. Since it was built in 1973, it has received world wide notice. Facing Sydney's beautiful harbor, the soaring roofs swell upward like the giant sails of a great ship of the seas. Along with this famous building, Australia has produced some world famous opera singers, including Marjorie Lawrence, Dame Nellie Melba, and Dame Joan Sutherland. Famous composers from Australia include Percy Grainger, Peter Sculthorpe, and Richard Meale. Although very proud of its own musical artists, Australia has built a concert hall known for its international flavor. It was designed by the Danish architect Jorn Utzan and has featured performances of works by many of the world's great composers. Your first visit to Australia should include a concert, opera, or ballet at the Sydney Opera House.

Choose to do one of the following and share it with the class.

- Make a list of all the instruments used in a modem symphony orchestra. Include a sketch of each.

- Make a diagram of a concert stage, showing where most symphony orchestras group the various instruments for their performances.

- Make a list of the most famous symphony orchestras in the world and their most famous conductors. You may illustrate your list with drawings or pictures of orchestra instruments.

- Following is a short list of international composers whose works have been presented in the Sydney Opera House. Research one and write a report to the class.

Austria:	Gustave Mahler, Johann Strauss, Joseph Haydn, Wolfgang Mozart
British:	Sir Edward Elgar, Frederick Delius, Benjamin Britten
French:	Hector Berlioz, Georges Bizet, Claude Debussy, Jules Massenet
United States:	Aaron Copland, Charles Ives, George Gershwin

- Use the following words for a spelling challenge: symphony, orchestra, ballet, violin, concert.

Visit a Game Preserve

Although surrounded by water, Australia is so large it is a continent, not just an island. Over 50 million years ago it was cut off from other land masses. Scientists think this is probably the reason Australia still has the world's largest number of the unusual mammals called **marsupials**. All marsupials have pouches for carrying their babies until they are old enough to survive outside. This is the main difference between marsupials and other mammals — the way babies are born. The word marsupial means "pouched" animal. Most other mammals give birth to "finished" babies that can survive outside. Over 170 different species of marsupials live in and around Australia. They come in all different colors, sizes, and shapes. These differences generally depend on where the animals live — deserts, rain forests, woods, or grasslands. The average male red kangaroo, for example, stands about six feet (1.8 meters) tall, while the smallest marsupial mouse is about 3 ¾ inches (9.5 cm.) long, including his tail. When you visit a game preserve here, you will be able to observe some of the most fascinating creatures of our world — the animals of Australia.

Match the marsupials on the right to their descriptions on the left.

A powerful jumper, the red kangaroo can leap 11 feet (3.3 m) and reach speeds of 40 miles (64 km) per hour on short distances.

The koala lives in eucalyptus trees, has two thumbs on his hands, and looks like a living teddy bear.

Living in underground burrows like a groundhog, the wombat likes to eat grass and lives in or near the edge of forests.

A long nose, a sticky tongue, strong claws — these belong to the banded anteater (numbat), which loves to feast on termites.

A medium-sized kangaroo, this animal is called the pretty-face wallaby. Can you tell why?

Camping Out in the Bush

After visiting the Sydney Opera House and a game preserve, you are ready to see another part of Australia — the "bush" or "outback" as the undeveloped parts of the country are called.

1. Before leaving, you will need to acquire some supplies — food, clothing, and equipment. You will be sleeping outdoors, cooking your own food, and you will be far from stores or cities. Individually or in small groups, complete the following chart of supplies. Plan your trip for seven days, including all food, clothes, and equipment (flashlight, sleeping bag, etc.) you will need. For each item listed, place an estimated cost in the proper column. When you have finished your plans, add all costs together for a grand total.

Bush Supply List

Item Needed	Amount	Estimated Cost
I. Food *(for 7 days)*		
_____	_____	_____
_____	_____	_____
_____	_____	_____
_____	_____	_____
_____	_____	_____
_____	_____	_____
_____	_____	_____
II. Clothing		
_____	_____	_____
_____	_____	_____
_____	_____	_____
_____	_____	_____
II. Equipment		
_____	_____	_____
_____	_____	_____
_____	_____	_____
_____	_____	_____
_____	_____	_____
_____	_____	_____
	Total Cost $	_____

Camping Out in the Bush *(cont.)*

2. On your first night sleeping under the stars, you may notice that the sky patterns look different from those in the northern hemisphere. You will not be able to see the Big Dipper, the Little Dipper, or the North Star. On the following diagram, see what major stars and constellations of the southern skies you can identify. Be sure to locate the Southern Cross, the famous grouping of stars that appears on the Australian flag.

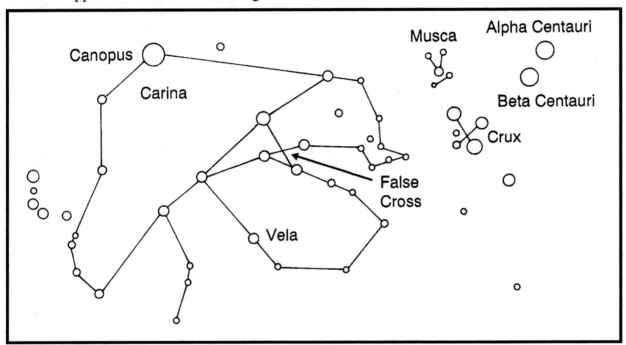

3. **Australian Aborigines:** On your camping trip into the bush, you might meet some of the most interesting of all Australian people — Aborigines, who have chosen to live in their traditional ways rather than move to the cities. Aborigines are native Australians whose ancestors were the first to live in the great island-continent. Scientists believe they have been there for 40,000 years. Aborigines lived in harmony with nature, hunting food and gathering plants. They lived outdoors, wore few clothes, and made stone tools like axes, clubs, and spearpoints. They were the ingenious inventors and skillful throwers of that clever instrument called the boomerang. Their ancient cave paintings and drawings are world-famous. Their rich tradition of music, song, and storytelling reveals a belief that the world was created ages ago in a period called Dreamtime. Their stories of the Dreamtime have added much to the world's treasury of myth and folktale. Many of these stories relate the origins of the animals of Australia. Perhaps you will meet an Aborigine who will tell you one of the stories his ancestors have passed down through the centuries by word of mouth.

In the tradition of storytelling, read orally "How the Platypuses Came to Australia" *(Best-Loved Folktales of the World,* selected by Joanna Cole, Anchor Books Doubleday, 1982) or "How Kangaroos Came to Australia," a story told by an Aborigine character in the novel *Thunderwith* by Libby Hathorn, Little, Brown and Company, 1989, pp. 99-100. Do this with lots of feeling and imagination.

Once you have finished, create your own imaginative folktale explaining the origin of an unusual Australian animal. Combine the class tales into a class book. Illustrate your folktale.

The Australian Outback

Most Australians today live in large modern cities along the southeast coast. Many others live farther west in the great plains and deserts of central Australia on the famous sheep and cattle stations (ranches). These stations can often be huge. In fact, one of them is said to be 12,000 square miles (31,080 sq. km) in size. (In the United States, the XIT ranch in Texas was 5,000 square miles.) Imagine how much livestock might graze in such an area! Of course, this also means that many of the families in the outback are quite isolated, far from towns, doctors, schools, or even other families. Because of this, some children do not "go" to school. They do their lessons at home and talk to their teachers by radio. Also, the families must be prepared with proper first aid equipment in case of illness or accident. On your camping trip, you might see an Australian sheep or cattle station.

Imagine you are an Australian living in the outback on a large sheep station.

1. **Outback Emergency:** Make up a complete list of the first aid and medical supplies you will need to take care of emergencies until you can reach a doctor who is over one hundred miles away.

2. **Outback Teacher:** Choose another student as a partner. One is to be the teacher, and one to be the student. Then choose a recent science lesson or experiment you did in class. (Your teacher will help you select some appropriate lessons.) Together with your partner write a dialogue of what an outback "radio teacher" might say to teach this lesson or explain this experiment. Be sure to include what the student might ask when he or she does not understand. Remember that neither one can see the other. In fact, it might help to turn your backs to one another or set a screen between yourselves while writing the dialogue. All directions, questions, and explanations must be given in very clear wording, since no demonstrations or illustrations can take place. After all dialogues are completed, trade your radio lessons with another team and check to see if your dialogue will work to teach another person your lesson.

The Great Barrier Reef

Your last adventure before leaving Australia will be to visit one of the great wonders of the world — The Great Barrier Reef.

The Great Barrier Reef is sometimes called the largest living thing in the world. It is actually a series of coral reefs that stretch for 1250 miles (2010 km) along the northeast coast of Australia. Coral reefs are made of the hardened skeletons of dead sea animals along with living coral polyps in colors of blue, green, purple, red, and yellow. The limestone formation on which all of this exists lies under or just above the surface of the sea. Because of the many colorful animals living along The Great Barrier Reef, it seems like a beautiful water garden. It supports nearly 1500 species of fish, along with many birds, crabs, giant clams, and sea turtles. Many of these creatures have colorful names that describe their appearance. See how many of the following you can identify in the coral reef below. You may color the reef later.

a. Porcupine Puffer

b. Hawksbill Turtle

c. Sea Urchin

d. Staghorn Coral

e. Sea Star

f. Fan Coral

g. Sponge

h. Elkhorn Coral

i. Brain Coral

j. Four-eyed Butterfly Fish

k. Queen Angelfish

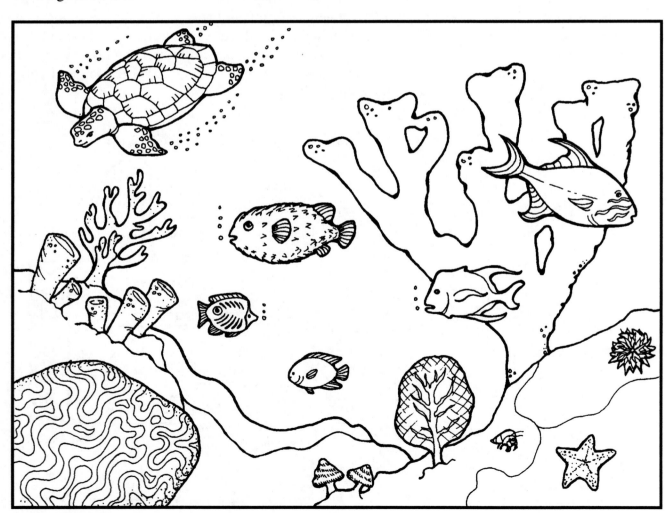

China

1. **Map of China,** page *50*

   Discuss the country's location, borders, geographical

   Extending Activities:

   Assign group reports on the following topics:
   * History
   * Art of China

2. **Facts About China; Chinese Words and Phrases,** page 51

   Extending Activities:
   * Have students color the flag.
   * Assign reports as suggested on page 4.
   * Practice saying the Chinese words and phrases. Ask students to use them in sentences.

3. **Practice Using Chopsticks,** page 52.

   Extending Activities:
   * Prepare rice in class. Practice eating it with chopsticks.
   * Have a meal at a Chinese restaurant.

4. **Chinese Characters,** page 53

   Extending Activities:
   * Practice writing the characters. Write a greeting card.

5. **Abacus,** pages 54-55

   Extending Activities:
   * Give some math problems letting students use their abacuses to solve them.

6. **Find out about the giant panda.**

   Extending Activities:
   * Make a fan with a panda on it.
   * Make a poster explaining why the panda is endangered and what we can do to help.
   * Serve canned bamboo shoots.

7. **The Chinese Zodiac Signs,** page 56

   Extending Activities:
   * Discuss a lunar calendar.
   * Find out about the animals that the calendar represents.

8. **Chinese Theater**

   Extending Activities:
   * Talk about Chinese drama. The Yuan dynasty from 1279-1368 saw the beginning of formal drama. A combination of dialog, songs, dance, colorful costumes, and symbolic gestures constitutes the Beijing opera, or Peking opera, which has been the most popular form of theater in China since the 1800s. These operas are based on stories, history, and folktales of China. Take a Chinese folktale and create a play. Present it to the class.

9. **Raise silk worms.**
   * Check for videos or filmstrips on silk weaving. Discuss metamorphosis and draw the life cycle.

10. **Design and make a kite.**

    Extending Activities:
    * Attend or hold your own kite festival.
    * Discuss the wind as a source of power. Brainstorm objects that are moved by the wind and discuss the sounds made by the wind.

11. **Discuss the Great Wall of China.**

    Extending Activities:
    * Find out why the Great Wall of China was built. (It was constructed to keep invaders out of central Asia.)
    * The wall is about 4,600 miles (7,400 km) long. Have students do some math problems using these numbers. Let them figure out how far away a trip of that length would take them from where they live.
    * Make a model of the Great Wall.

12. **Printing Blocks,** page 57

    Extending Activities:
    * Make cards using printing blocks.

13. **Celebrate the Chinese New Year,** page 58

    Extending Activities
    * Read dragon stories.
    * Brainstorm using similes such as "A dragon is as big as . . ."
    * Write a poem about a dragon.

Bibliography

Nonfiction

Baskin, Hosie. *A Book of Dragons.* (Knopf, 1985)

Bonners, Susan. *Panda.* (Dell, 1988)

Brown, Tricia. *The Chinese New Year.* (Henry Holt, 1987)

Fritz, Jean. *China Homecoming.* (Putnam, 1985)

McLenighan, Valjean. *China, a History to 1949.* (Childrens Press, 1983)

McLenighan, Valjean. *People's Republic of China.* (Childrens Press, 1984)

Nesbit, Edith. *The Book of Dragons.* (Dell, 1986)

Yu, Ling. *Cooking the Chinese Way.* (Lerner, 1982)

Fiction

Grahame, Kenneth. *The Reluctant Dragon.* (Henry Holt, 1988)

Heyer, Marilee. *The Weaving of a Dream.* (Puffin, 1989)

Mosel, Arlene. *Tikki Tikki Tembo.* (Henry Holt, 1992)

Yep, Laurence. *Dragon Steel.* (HarperCollins, 1985)

Yolen, Jane. *The Emperor and the Kite.* (Putnam, 1988)

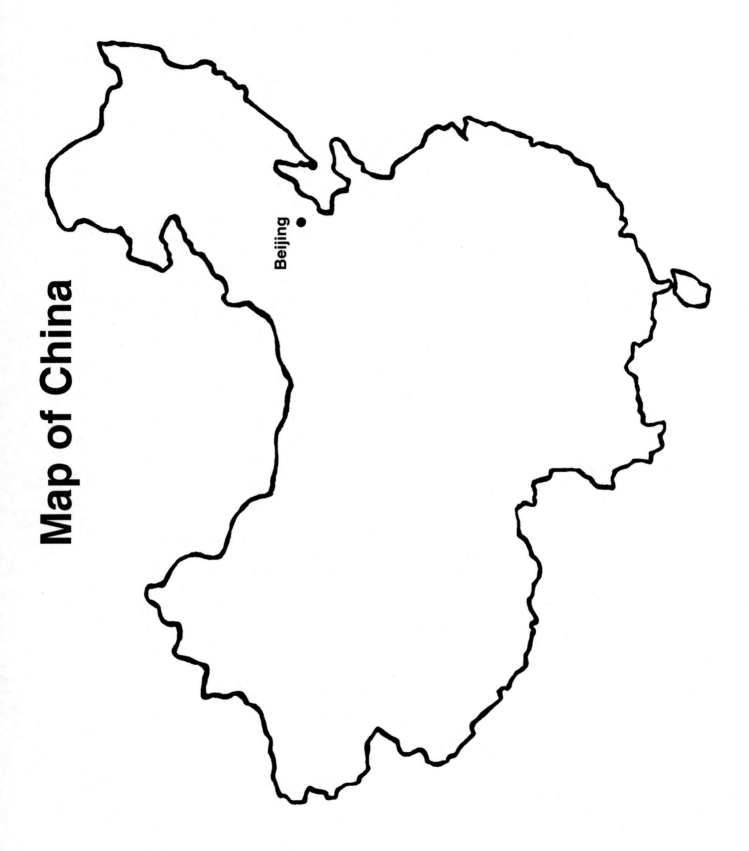

Map of China

Beijing

Facts About China

Capital:	Beijing
Largest city:	Shanghai
Language:	Mandarin
Currency:	Yuan
Population:	1,273,111,000
Area:	3,969,032 sq. mi. (9,572,678 sq. km)
Agriculture:	Cabbage, corn, cotton, fruits, potatoes, rice
Industry:	Cement, textiles, iron, steel, petroleum, food processing
Flag colors:	Red with one large yellow star and four small ones

Mandarin Chinese Words and Phrases

dzau-an	Good morning
wu-an	Good afternoon
wan-an	Good evening
nin hau	Hello
sye-sye	Thank you
ching	Please
nin gwei-sying?	What is your name?
wo ming . . .	My name is
ji	Chicken
my an-bau	Bread

Write three other words or phrases you would like to learn in Mandarin.

_____

_____

_____

Using Chopsticks

In China there are two utensils used to eat with: soup spoons and chopsticks. Kuai-tse or chopsticks are used instead of forks. For those used to eating with forks, chopsticks can provide a new experience in eating. Obtain some chopsticks. They are often available at Chinese restaurants or in the foreign food sections of supermarkets. If no chopsticks are available, try practicing with unsharpened pencils. Follow these directions.

1. Place one chopstick in your hand, laying the stick between your thumb and index finger. This chopstick will stay still; don't let it move.

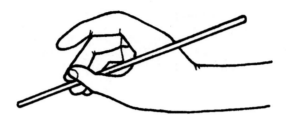

2. Use your thumb, index finger and two middle fingers to hold the second chopstick. The chopstick will move to pick up the food.

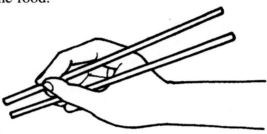

3. Keep the bottom points of the chopsticks even. Move the second chopstick to "pinch" the food against the first chopstick. Pick up the food.

A Chopstick Game

To play this game you will need chopsticks, seeds or dried beans, small containers, and a timer.

Set several seeds or dried lima beans out on a table. Set the timer for one minute. Using chopsticks, pick up seeds or lima beans. Place them in a small container. The person with the most in the container is the winner.

Chinese Characters

People in China speak in many different dialects of the same language. There are so many different pronunciations that the dialects are considered to be separate languages. The official language of China is Northern Chinese. Non-Chinese people call this language Mandarin, while in China is referred to as *putonghua,* or common language.

Even though Chinese is spoken in so many different ways, it is written the same. It uses a system of characters instead of an alphabet.

Look at the Chinese characters below and what they stand for. Practice writing each character on scratch paper. After you have mastered them, write them in the box below each character.

Then write a story using some of the characters. Exchange your paper with another student and let him/her try reading your story.

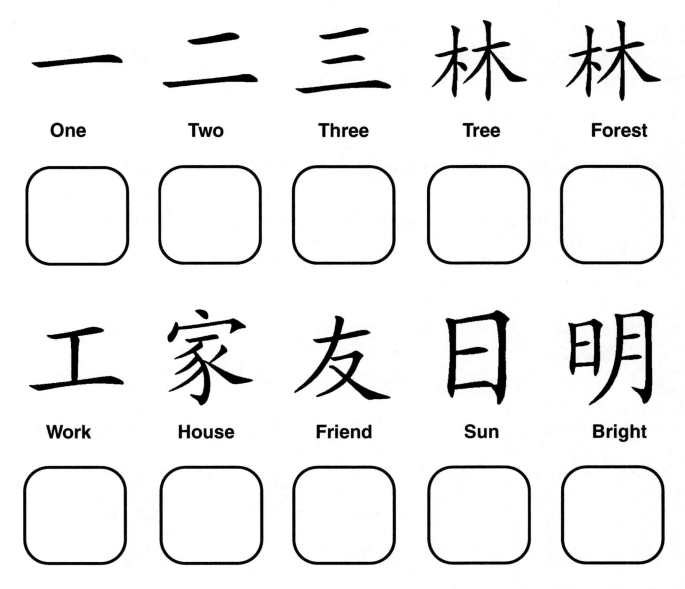

一　　二　　三　　林　　林

One　　**Two**　　**Three**　　**Tree**　　**Forest**

工　　家　　友　　日　　明

Work　　**House**　　**Friend**　　**Sun**　　**Bright**

Abacus

An abacus is a tool for counting and doing simple arithmetic. It is the forerunner of our modern calculators and computers. The abacus is still used around the world, with each country having its own name and style for it.

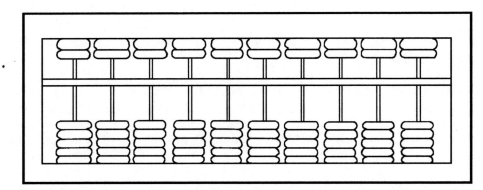

In China, the abacus is called suan-pan, which means counting tray. This Chinese abacus has rods with five beads below and two beads above a crossbar within a wooden or plastic frame. The beads on top are called the heaven beads and the lower ones are called the earth beans.

Make your own suan-pan and learn how easy adding and subtracting can be by using this simple number machine.

To make an abacus you will need:

> 1 shoebox lid, a strip of cardboard 1" (2.54 cm) wide and length of the lid; 6-8 pieces of string at least 2" (5 cm) longer than the side of the lid; beads or "O" shaped cereal or salad macaroni— 7 per string; tape; scissors

Tape the 1" (2.54 cm) strip of cardboard in a standing position inside the lid approximately 2" (5 cm) from one edge to create a horizontal divider for the beads.

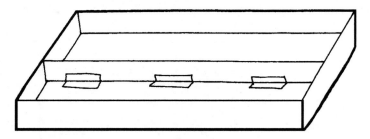

Cut six to eight ½" (1.3 cm) slits approximately 1" (2.54 cm) apart along the top and bottom edges and the cardboard divider. Then string beads on each string, and place them into the slits so that 2 beads are above the divider and 5 are below. Tape the ends of the strings to the lid.

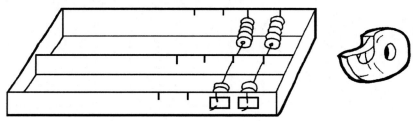

Abacus *(cont.)*

Now you are ready to use your new abacus. Each column of beads is like the "places" in our number system. The lower, or earth beads, are each worth 1 and the upper, or heaven beads, are each worth 5. Begin with all the beads moved away from the divider—heaven beads up and earth beads down. Choose any column to work with as the "ones" place. To show a number such as 3, simply move three earth beads up. To show the number 7, move one heaven bead down and two earth beads up.

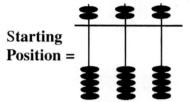
Starting Position =

3=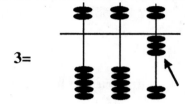

7=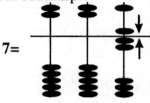

How do you think you would show the number 39? If you moved three earth beads up in the next column to the left, you are absolutely right. Which column would you use to show 300? Read the number on the picture abacuses below. Then try placing number 33, 77, 4, 146, 908, and 21 on your own abacus. (Be sure to clear the abacus between each number for this practice.)

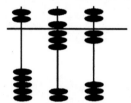 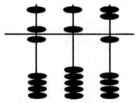 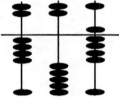

Now let's try some simple arithmetic. To add 25 + 12, place 25 on the abacus. Then, without clearing the bead, place 12 more. Look at the resulting number Does it say 37?

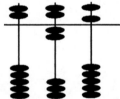 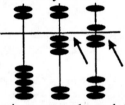

If at any time both heaven beads in a column are used up, just carry 1 earth bead up in the next column to take their place and clear those two heaven beads back away. For example, 7 + 5:

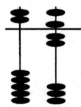 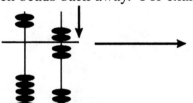 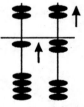

To subtract, simply take away the second number of beads. Try 44-13. Your abacus should show:

Try a variety of other addition and subtraction problems. Sometimes you may have to "borrow" from a higher column by exchanging a higher earth bead for two lower heaven beads to be able to do the subtraction.

Chinese Zodiac Signs

The Chinese calendar is based on a lunar calendar which actually began in 2637 B.C. At that time, Emperor Huang Ti, who had reigned for 61 years, introduced a 60 year cycle that is made up of five 12-year cycles. Those five cycles correspond to the five elements: wood, fire, earth, metal, and water. Legend says that Lord Buddha called all the animals to him before he left the earth but only 12 came to say good-bye. As a reward for coming, Buddha named a year after each animal in the order that it arrived. These were: 1. Rat, 2. Ox, 3. Tiger, 4. Rabbit, 5. Dragon, 6. Snake, 7. Horse, 8. Sheep, 9. Monkey, 10. Rooster, 11. Dog, and 12. Boar. The animals are said to influence the year's events as well as the personalities of those born in that year.

Using the Chinese Lunar Calendar below, complete the following activity.

Make a list of five people you know who are different ages including yourself. Find out the year that they were born. Then read the calendar below and find out in the year of what animal each was born. Look at the characteristics. Do they seem to fit you or the people listed?

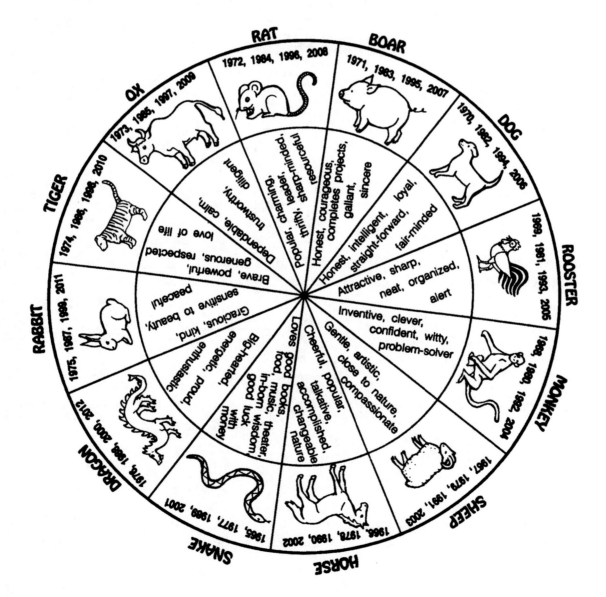

Chinese Printing Blocks

Block printing was probably invented in China more than 2000 years ago. Character and pictures were carved onto wood blocks, inked, and then transferred to paper.

Although moveable type was invented in 1045 by Bi sheng, it did not have much development in China. This was because the Chinese language has thousands of characters, which would have made it very difficult to move type. Instead, wood block printing became a popular way of reproduction.

Activity

Make a wood block print. You will need scissors, water-based printing ink, craft sticks or paper clips, two foam meat trays, small sponge, brayer or roller, drawing paper.

1. Trim the edges from one of the foam trays to create a rectangle. Sketch an idea backwards on the smooth side. It may be an original design or Chinese characters. (See page 53.)
2. When you have finished sketching, use the craft stick or paper clip to "carve" in your design.
3. Place a small amount of printing ink into a foam meat tray. Roll the brayer in the ink, then roll the ink covered brayer over the "carved" design.
4. Place the drawing paper over the inked design. Press firmly and evenly over it. Peel the paper off the inked design.
5. Use your print to create a card or wall hanging.

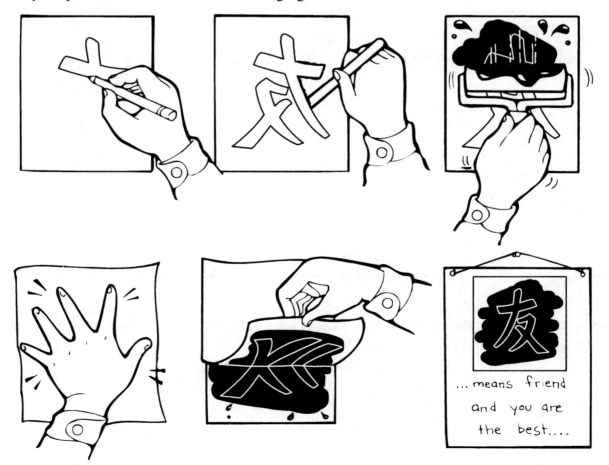

Dragons and the Chinese New Year

The Chinese New Year is celebrated in late January or early February. It changes because it is based on a lunar calendar. In preparation for the celebration, houses are cleaned, new clothes are purchased, special foods are prepared, and the colors of joy, red and orange, are seen everywhere.

Parades featuring the Chinese dragon are held. The dragon was considered sacred and was a symbol of the Chinese emperor. It stood for strength and goodness.

Celebrate the Chinese New Year. Start by decorating your room with paper lanterns. Then make a dragon for a big parade. Parade through the classroom and your school.

Paper Lanterns

Cut strips leaving 1" (2.54 cm) at the top and bottom uncut. Tape the side together. A handle can be made from a paper strip and streamers can be attached to the bottom of the lantern.

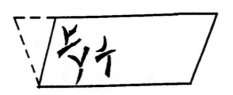

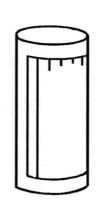
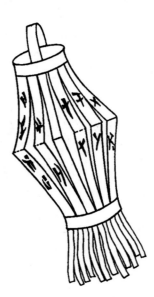

Dragon

Make a dragon using boxes or paper sacks. Make the head of the dragon first, drawing a face on it. Then color it in. Make the body by using sacks or boxes that are decorated with crayons, fabric scraps, or crepe paper streamers. Make as many body segments as you wish. Connect the body pieces to each other and then the head. Staples will work for paper sacks. A heavy duty stapler, rope, or heavy duty tape will connect the boxes. Add a tail using crepe paper streamers or long strips of cloth. Parade around holding the dragon up over your head.

Japan

1. **Map of Japan,** page 60

   Discuss the country's location, borders, geographical features, climate, and cities.

   Extending Activities:

   Assign group reports on the following topics:

   • History, earthquakes, literatures, theater

2. **Facts About Japan, Japanese Words and Phrases,** page 61

   Have students color the flag.

   Assign reports as suggested on page 4.

   Practice saying the Japanese words and phrases. Ask students to use them in sentences.

3. **Japanese Customs in the Home,** page 62

   Extending Activities:

   • Ask some questions about the reasoning behind certain customs such as removing shoes before entering a home.

   • Make an oriental screen on a piece of paper folded into three sections. Decorate it. Fold on the section lines so that it stands like a screen.

   • Research a traditional tea ceremony and perform it.

4. **Flower Arranging,** page 63

   Extending Activities:

   • Find out what type of flowers grow in Japan. Try growing some in your classroom.

   • Investigate the art of bonsai.

5. **Earthquakes!,** page 64

   Extending Activities:

   • Discuss volcanoes.

   • Find out about what causes earthquakes.

6. **Try some Japanese art forms.**

   • Try some origami, the art of paper folding.

   • Use a paint brush and ink to draw basic strokes of Japanese characters.

7. **Tanka and Haiku,** page 65

   • Find out about some Japanese poets and authors. Read some of their writings.

8. **Japanese Festivals,** page 66

   Extending Activity:

   • Make a Japanese Good Luck Tree. Take a twig _with branches and put it in a tin can. Fill the can with dirt to hold it in place. Decorate the tree with Japanese good luck symbols like goldfish and insects. Add yarn to decorate.

9. **Fishing in Japan**

   • Explain that Japan is one of the greatest fishing countries. Japan catches $\frac{1}{6}$ of the world's fish.

   • Find out about how cormorants are used to help in fishing.

   • Research oyster farming in Japan.

10. **Take a trip on the bullet train.**

    • Tokaido, the bullet train, travels at 120 miles per hour. Do some math problems asking students where they would be 120 miles from home.

Bibliography

Nonfiction

Greene, Carol. *Japan.* (Children's Press, 1983)

Kalman, Bobbie. *Japan, the Culture.* (Crabtree, 1989)

Kalman, Bobbie. *Japan, the Land.* (Crabtree, 1989)

Kalman, Bobbie. *Japan, the People.* (Crabtree, 1989)

Tames, Richard. *Japan: The Land and Its People.* (Lerneer, 1987)

Fiction

Coatsworth, Elizabeth. *The Cat Who Went to Heaven.* (Macmillan, 1990)

Mosel, Arlene. *The Funny Little Woman.* (Dutton, 1972)

Map of Japan

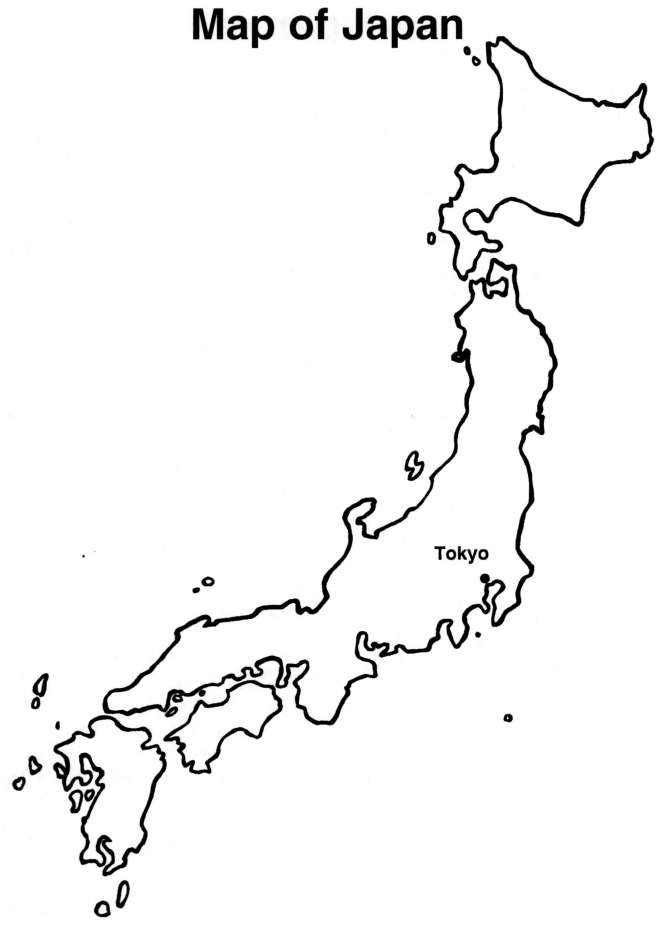

Tokyo

Facts About Japan

Capital:	Tokyo
Largest city:	Tokyo
Language:	Japanese
Currency:	Yen
Population:	126,771,000
Area:	145,870 sq. mi. (377,801 sq. km)
Agriculture:	Rice, vegetables, fruit, sugar beets, wheat, hogs
Industry:	Fishing, autos, calculators, computers, electronics, iron, steel, coal
Flag colors:	White with red circle

Japanese Words and Phrases

Ohayoo gozairnasu	Good morning
Konnichi wa	Good afternoon
Komban wa	Good evening
Sayonara	Goodbye
Ogenki desu ka	How are you?
hai/fie	Yes/No
pan	bread
tomodachi	friend
Sore wa ikura desu ka	How much is that?
tabemono	food
mizu	water

Write three other words or phrases that you want to learn in Japanese:

_____

_____

_____

Japanese Customs in the Home

In Japanese homes, there are several customs observed. Read about some of them. When you have finished, read through the questions. Think about your answers before you write them down.

A traditional Japanese home is a very private place. It is for family members, and guests aren't usually entertained in it. However, a guest bows to his or her host upon entering.

The structure itself is made from wood. *Fusuma* or sliding paper doors inside the house divide are it. These doors can be arranged so that there are many rooms or one large one. The floors are covered with *tatami*. Tatami are mats woven out of rice straw. They are all a standard size. Room measurements are based on how many mats it takes to cover the floor.

A bed consists of a foam mattress placed on the tatami, that is then covered with a thin cotton mattress called a futon. A fluffy quilt, also called a futon, is placed on the bed.

When entering a Japanese home, shoes are removed. People sit on the floor using *zabuton* or small cushions. There may be screens placed in the house.

The house has a small kitchen because food is purchased fresh each day. The kitchen contains an electric rice cooker since rice is part of almost every meal.

Baths are used for soaking and relaxation. All the washing up is done before someone enters the bathtub. The whole family may use the same water to wash.

1. How do the Japanese greet each other? How do people in the West greet each other?

   _____

2. Why might it be important for a house to be divided up quickly? Into what rooms would you divide a house?

   _____

3. How are the rooms measured? What information would you need to know if you had to know the area of a room in meters or yards?

   _____

4. Why are tatami mats given in standard sizes?

   _____

5. How is a bed in a traditional Japanese home different than yours?

   _____

6. Why do you think people remove their shoes when entering a Japanese home?

   _____

7. Would a large refrigerator be necessary in a Japanese house? Support your answer.

   _____

Flower Arranging

In Japan, flower arranging is an art In the 500s, Japanese Buddhists made elaborate floral arrangements for their temples. As the years have progressed the arrangements have been simplified.

Japanese floral arrangements are created to look natural. The flowers are supposed to look as if they were growing outdoors. Design and color are used to achieve this look. Stems and leaves play a major part in the arrangement. The tallest flowers in the arrangements represent heaven, the middle flowers represent man, and the lower flowers represent the earth.

Activity

Make a flower arrangement of your own. You will need flowers with leaves, a vase, scissors, and water if using fresh flowers. If fresh flowers aren't available, use artificial flowers or make some of your own.

To make your own flowers you will need pipe cleaners, construction paper or egg cups, tape, and glue. Use these to create flowers. Be sure to make the stems (pipe cleaners) are different lengths.

Before actually working with the flowers, sketch how you would like your flower arrangement to look when completed. Remember to emphasize the leaves and stems. Try putting the flowers at different levels. After you are satisfied with your sketch, try arranging the flowers. You may find that your flowers still need some more arranging.

Take your time and make your arrangement as lovely as possible.

Display your flowers.

Earthquakes!

There is an ancient legend in Japan. This legend says that Japan is the back of an old, sleepy dragon. When the dragon moves in its sleep, earthquakes occur.

Japan has had some devastating earthquakes. The worst one took place on September 1, 1923. The earthquake hit at noon, just as people were lighting fires to prepare their lunches on small braziers. The cities of Tokyo and Yokohama were left in ruins, with over a hundred thousand people dead. Most of the damage done was caused by these fires.

Japan is constantly shifting. It lies on a very unstable part of the earth's crust. There are as many as 1,500 earthquakes a year. Many of these are minor and cause no damage. However, some earthquakes occur underwater. They may result in a tsunami, which is a gigantic, destructive, massive wave.

Although there is no known way to stop an earthquake, people can be prepared for them. In Japan, regularly scheduled earthquake drills take place. People turn off their electric heaters and gas stoves. They take cover under tables. Many homes have earthquake survival kits.

Activity

With a small group of classmates plan an earthquake survival kit for your classroom. You must have enough food, water, and supplies to survive for 72 hours.

Some things to consider before you plan are where will you store your kit, what medical supplies would be important, and how can food stay safe for eating. You do not need to consider price.

Brainstorm and write down your ideas here. After you have finished, compare your answers with the class. Did you come up with the same items for your kits?

_____   _____   _____

_____   _____   _____

_____   _____   _____

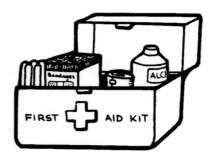

Tanka and Haiku

There are two very old forms of Japanese poetry that still exist today. Tanka, which is a 31-syllable poem written in a strict pattern was first written in the 700s. It is the earliest collection of poetry and contains more than 4,500 poems. Most of the poems are tankas whose themes are of love, nature, and friendship.

In what is referred to as the Tokugawa period in literature from 1603 to 1867, a new form of verse called a haiku became popular. The original haikus were 17-syllable poems that were comic in nature. However, in the 1600s a poet named Matuso Basho wrote haiku and became responsible for it becoming a serious art form. These poems followed a strict format and were about nature. Because they are so spare in their language, it is left to the reader to interpret the poems.

Activity

Try your hand at writing a tanka and a haiku. The syllable patterns along with a sample for each are given below. The tanka's subject must be love, nature, or friendship, while the haiku should be a subject about nature. When you are through, copy your poems over and illustrate them.

Tanka

The red leaves dangle *(5 syllables)*

About to fall, but not quite *(7 syllables)*

Ready for descent *(5 syllables)*

They prefer to linger on *(7 syllables)*

Content in the peaceful breeze *(7 syllables)*

Haiku

Raindrops like bubbles *(5 syllables)*

Clinging to each leaf like glue *(7 syllables)*

Even upside down *(5 syllables)*

Japanese Festivals

Children hold a special place in Japan. So special are Japanese children that there are festivals, or matsuris to honor them. May 5th is a double holiday. On this day both Children's Day and Boys' Day is celebrated. The Boys' Day Festival is hundreds of years old, while Children's Day became a national holiday in 1948. Traditionally, a bamboo pole with fish-shaped wind socks or paper streamers representing the sons in the household are flown above the house in order of the oldest to youngest son, with the sizes varying accordingly.

On March 3rd, the Japanese celebrate Hina Matusuri, which is the Doll Festival. This is a special day for girls. Special dolls called Hina dolls are displayed. They are not played with, but displayed in a special way. They sit on graduated shelves covered in red. On the top sit the emperor and empress. Under them are three ladies in waiting, and then five musicians, two officials, and three guardsmen. The display also includes furniture, food offerings, cakes, and candies.

Shichi-Go-San is celebrated on November 15th. The festival is called "Seven-Five-Three." On this day 3-or 5-year old boys and girls of 3 or 7 dress in their finest clothes, either traditional kimonos or western-style dress. They are given a narrow, colorful decorated bag. The bags show symbols of youth and long life such as the tortoise or crane. The families go to their place of worship or shrine and give thanks for the health and happiness of their children. The children are given toys and gifts in their paper bags and may even have a party.

Activity

In honor of Boys' Day, make a fish wind sock. You will need one full, folded sheet of plain newsprint, tape, string, wire, crayon, glue or paste, scissors, stick or dowel.

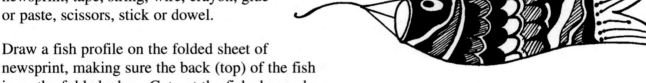

Draw a fish profile on the folded sheet of newsprint, making sure the back (top) of the fish is on the folded edge. Cut out the fish shape; do not cut the fold. Open the fish and lay it flat. Add additional fins, if desired. Use crayons to decorate the fish, making each side the same. Fold and glue the top and bottom edges of the fish closed. Do not glue mouth, Stuff loosely with newspaper wads through the tail opening. Glue the tail closed. To strengthen the mouth, tape a piece of wire (wire will allow you to shape the mouth) along the inside mouth edge; then fold the edge of the paper over the wire mouth twice and glue down. Shape the mouth. Tape the ends of three 6" (15 cm) pieces of string to the mouth opening. Tie the other ends together. Tie one end of a longer piece of string to the 6" (15 cm) strings. Attach the long string to a stick or dowel which will be used to hold the fish kite.

- In honor of Hina Matsuri, make dolls or bring them from home. Display them in your class.
- In honor of Shichi-Go-San, work with a preschool or little "buddy class." Decorate lunch sacks for the children and fill them with treats. Plan a party that includes games and songs that you can teach and play with them.

India

1. **Map of India,** page 68

   Discuss the country's location, borders, geographical features, climate, and cities.

   Extending Activities:

   Assign group reports on the following topics:

   - Geographical features of the country including the importance of the Ganges River.
   - Common festivals and celebrations
   - The importance of the dance in India

2. **Facts About India; Hindi Words and Phrases,** page 69

   Have students color the flag.

   Assign reports as suggested on page 4.

   Practice saying the Hindi words and phrases. Ask students to use them in sentences.

3. **Find out about New Dehli.**

   - Do some research about the sights of New Dehli including the Parliament House, President's Palace, and the Red Fort.

4. **Compare the Religions of India,** page 70

   Extending Activities:

   - Make a model of a mosque.
   - Discuss the beliefs of the Hindus.
   - Find out rules regarding treatment of animals.
   - In small groups, discuss what these rules represent.
   - Investigate the caste system.

5. **The Taj Mahal,** page 71

   Extending Activities:

   - Find examples of Moguhl architecture.
   - Explain the design and decoration of the Taj Mahal.

6. **Sitar Music,** page 72

   Extending Activities:

   - Find out about other types of Indian instruments.
   - Explore Indian dance that includes use of the performers arms, hands, and fingers to tell a story.
   - Listen to some Indian music and create dances.

7. **Make shadow puppets.**

   Extending activities:

   - Write and perform a play about good King Rama, the protector of the weak and poor, and his beautiful queen, Sita, and their fight against Ravan, the evil demon king.

   - Read some Indian folktales and make up some other plays.

8. **Locate the Ganges River on a map.**

   Find out why the Ganges is considered sacred.

9. **Elephant Problem Solving,** page 73

   Extending Activities:

   - Elephants are dressed in a small house called howdah. Find out about the howdah and draw a picture of an elephant wearing one.
   - Find out about game preserves in India.
   - Learn about cobras and snake charmers.

10. **It's Off to the Movies,** page 74

    Extending Activities:

    - Find out more about the Indian movie industry.
    - Research who the major motion picture stars are in India and how the movies affect the general population.

11. **Play a game of Pachisi.**

    Extending Activities:

    - The game of Pachisi is an ancient game of India. Find the a modern boxed game version or create your own set and play.
    - Find out about other games that are played in India.

12. **Discuss the current government in India.**

    Extending Activities:

    - Research the British rule in India and its influence on the country.

Bibliography

Nonfiction

Madavan, Vijay. *Cooking the Indian Way.* (Lerner, 1985)

Map of India

New Delhi

Facts About India

Capital:	New Delhi
Largest city:	Calcutta
Language:	Hindi, English, Sanskrit
Currency:	Rupee
Population:	1,000,000,000
Area:	1,269,346 sq.mi. (3,287,590 sq. km)
Agriculture:	Bananas, beans, chickpeas, cotton, potatoes, rice
Industry:	Brassware, silverware, textiles, iron, steel
Flag colors:	Top—orange, Middle—white with blue wheel, Bottom—green

Hindi Words and Phrases

Note: Hindi, English, and Sanskrit are all official languages of India. There are 13 regional languages.

na-mas-te	Hello or Goodbye
dhan-ya-vaad	Thanks
kai-se hain	How are you?
me-raa naam [John] hai.	My name is [John].
aap kaa naam kyaa hai	What is your name?
Da-bal ro-tee	bread
mur-gee	chicken
pair	foot
pi-taa	Father
sha-her	the city

Write three other words or phrases you would like to learn in Hindi.

_____

_____

_____

Major Religions of India

The two major religions in India are Hinduism and Islam.

These two religions play an important part in how the country is run. Using resources such as encyclopedias or reference books, find out more about the two religions. Then compare and contrast the two and fill in the chart below. After filling in the chart, use the information to write a paragraph below about the two religions and their influence on India.

	Hinduism	**Islam**
Percentage of population		
Dietary restrictions		
Sacred writings		
Buildings		
Marriage customs		
Clothing		
Festivals		

_____

_____

_____

_____

_____

_____

_____

The Taj Mahal

In Agra, in northern India, stands one of the most costly and beautiful tombs in the world, the Taj Mahal. It took about 20,000 workers approximately 20 years, from 1630-1650, to build this tomb. It was built in memory of Mumtaz Mahal, who died in 1629. She was the favorite wife of the Indian ruler, Shah Jahan. Mumtaz Mahal and Shah Jahan's tombs are in the basement of this monument.

The Taj Mahal is built of gleaming white marble, inlaid with semi-precious stones. It rests on white marble surrounded by four minarets.

Decorations consisting of floral patterns cover the walls. There are intricate inlays and relief carvings of floral design.

Activity

Recreate a pattern in clay similar to one found on the Taj Mahal. Since there are flowers and semi-precious stones found throughout this magnificent building, you will have the opportunity to design a tile similar to one found there.

Materials: patterns below, clay, roller, sequins or fancy buttons, tools to work in clay

Directions: Prepare clay by rolling it out and cutting it into a square or rectangle. Study some of the floral patterns below. Choose one or create one of your own. Then transfer the design to the clay. This can be done by tracing over the patterns onto the clay. Once the pattern is transferred, use some tools such as pencils or toothpicks to inscribe the pattern into the clay. You may also add detail to the pattern. Use sequins or buttons to simulate jewels.

The Music of the Sitar

The sitar, a popular instrument in India, had its beginnings in Persia or India. The sitar is one of the main instruments of classical music of northern India. This instrument has a long, broad neck made of wood and a pear-shaped body made from a large gourd. There are seven main strings that are plucked with a wire pick. Most of these strings create the melody. There are also another set of 12 sympathetic strings. When the main strings are played, these vibrate although they are not touched. Frets, adjustable metal strips, are attached to the neck of the sitar serving as a guide for fingering.

Activity

For this activity, you will need recordings of sitar music and western classical music. Two sources of this type of music are *Music of Ravi Shankar* on Ocora Records and *The Sounds of India* on Columbia Records.

Listen to a recording featuring sitar music and to another recording featuring western classical music. As you listen to both, take notes on what you are hearing. Consider some of the following: what instruments you hear and recognize, the rhythms, repetition of music, time or beat, and the emotions the music evokes.

When you have finished listening, look at your notes. Use them to create a list of questions. Exchange your questions with a fellow student. Then listen to the music again and have your classmate answer your questions. Use the questions to write a paragraph or two about the music and the comparisons between the two types of music.

Elephant Problem Solving

Tradition in ancient India called for respect of all forms of life. Today that is seen in the setting aside of land that forms wilderness areas. There are 247 wildlife sanctuaries and 53 national parks that the government has created for the wild animals of India.

These animals include bears, elephants, monkeys, yaks, wild birds, and tigers. The Bengal tiger, an endangered species, was the inspiration for Project Tiger begun in 1973. The program is dedicated to the preservation of these tigers and their natural habitats.

Asian or Indian elephants are also found in the forests and jungles of India. Elephants live in a matriarchal society. Families live with related females and their young. The oldest female heads the family.

Activity

There are many interesting numerical facts about elephants. Use the information given below to answer the questions. They will take more than just "figuring" them out.

1. The bull elephant stands 9 to 10 ½ feet tall (2.7 to 3.2 meters) and weighs approximately 8,000 pounds (3636 kg).

   a. How many classmates would it take to equal the height of an elephant?

   b. Weigh 5 textbooks. Determine how many textbooks would equal the weight of one elephant.

2. The tusk of a bull elephant measures 4 to 5 feet (1.2 to 1.5 meters).

   a. How many tusks would equal the area of your classroom? (Hint: area = length x width)

   b. How many inches or centimeters taller or shorter than an elephant's tusk are you?

3. The skin of an elephant is about 1½ inches (3 centimeters) thick and weighs about 2000 pounds (900 kg).

   a. How many sheets of paper are equal to the thickness of an elephant's skin?

   b. What fraction of the elephant's weight is its skin? (See problem #1).

4. An adult elephant's trunk can hold about 1½ gallons (6 liters) of water.

   a. How many cups (mL) of water can an elephant's trunk hold?

   b. How many gallons (liters) of water can an elephant's trunk hold?

5. Elephants can communicate with each other up to a distance of at least 2½ miles (4 kilometers).

   a. At what distance can you no longer communicate with a classmate?

It's Off to the Movies!

In modem India, the most popular form of entertainment is the movies. As a matter of fact, India produces more movies each year than any other country, making more than 800 hundred full-length features each year. Short features and documentaries are also made.

Bombay, Madras, and Calcutta are the primary movie-making areas. While most movies are shown within the country, many others are exported to foreign countries.

Activity

Make a movie. You will need a videocamera and videotape. As a class, choose a subject about India that you wish to explore further.

Divide the class into small groups. Working groups will include script writers and researchers, camera crew, prop and scene people, actors and actresses.

Before the script people meet, consider what you want your film to accomplish. Is it to teach something, will it be a travelogue, or strictly to entertain?

Once the script is written, the prop and scene people can prepare the necessary items. Parts can be assigned and practice can begin. The camera crew needs to practice using the video camera.

Before filming anything, have several rehearsals. When you are ready to film, make sure that it is during an uninterrupted block of time, and hang a sign on the door that says, "Do Not Disturb."

When the movie is completed, have a screening inviting other classes to join you on your trip around the world as you visit India.

Russia

1. **Map of Russia,** page 76

   Discuss the country's location, borders, geographical features, climate, and cities.

   Extending Activities:

   Assign groups on the following topics:

   - The current political situation
   - Communism in Russia
   - The arts

2. **Facts About Russia; Russian Words and Phrases,** page 77

   Have students color the flag.

   Assign reports as suggested on page 4.

   Practice saying the Russian words and phrases. Ask students to use them in sentences.

3. **Russian Names,** page 78

   Research how people and places get their names.

   Find out how names are changed through time.

4. **Famous Russians,** page 79

   As students find out about some famous Russians, have them share the information with the class.

5. **The Nutcracker,** page 80

   Extending Activities:

   - Research the Bolshoi or Kirov State Ballet.
   - Take a field trip to a ballet or have some dancers visit and give a performance.

6. **Listen to a recording of "Peter and the Wolf."**

   - Identify the instruments used.
   - Draw a favorite part of the story.
   - Write a different story using those same characters.
   - Read other Russian folktales.
   - Find out about Sergei Prokofiev.

7. **Make Matroyska dolls.**

   These are stacking dolls that are generally made out of brightly colored wood. Make Matroyska dolls using margarine tubs, boxes, or paper cups that nest into each other.

8. **A Space Mission,** page 81

   Extending Activities:

   - Discuss the history of the space race.
   - Follow the development of space vehicles such satellites to today; space shuttles.
   - Make diagrams showing development of rockets.
   - Build and launch homemade rockets.

9. **Russian Current Events**

   - Using magazine and newspaper articles, have students find out about the current political situation in Russia. Have them share and discuss the information.

Bibliography

Fiction
Robbins, Ruth. *Baboushka and the Three Kings.* (Houghton Mifflin, 1986)

Nonfiction
Hewitt, Phillip. *Looking at Russia.* (Harper, 1977)

Map of Russia

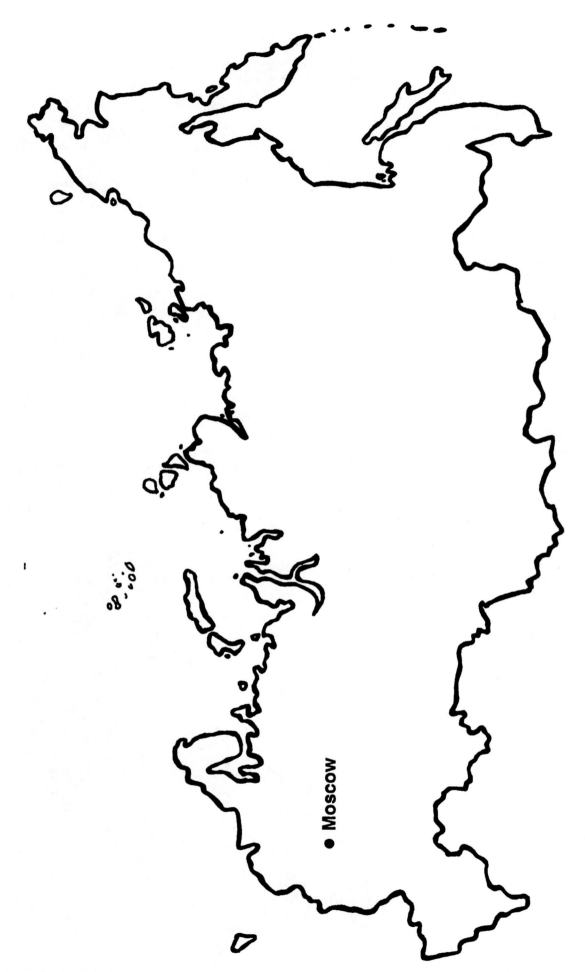

● Moscow

Facts About Russia

Capital:	Moscow
Largest city:	Moscow
Language:	Russian
Currency:	Ruble
Population:	145,470,000
Area:	6,592,850, sq. mi. (17,075,400 sq. km)
Agriculture:	Wheat, barley, oats, livestock, flax, fruits
Industry:	Fishing, chemicals, construction material, manufacturing, coal, motor vehicles
Flag colors:	Top—white, Middle—blue, Bottom—red

Russian Words and Phrases

do-bra-ye U-tra	Good Morning
do-briy d'en	Good Afternoon
do-bri-y v'e-chir	Good Evening
bal-shoy-e spa-s'i-ba	Thank you very much
pa-zha-la-ste	Please
kak pe-zhi-v A-yi-t'i	How are you?
kak va-she fa-m'il-ye?	What is your name?
ma-ya fa-m'il-ye . . .	My name is . . .
da	yes
n'et	no
avtomobil'	car
syr	cheese
noga	foot
kn'i-gu	book
mal'chik	boy
devochka	girl

Add three phrases or words you would like to learn in Russian.

_____

_____

_____

Russian Names

As in all countries, Russia has some favorite names. These names include:

Boys	**Girls**
Ivan (John)	Anna
Yuri (George)	Marya
Pavel (Paul)	Tatyana
Alexi	Ludmila

A son takes his father's name and adds -vich to it. So Pavel Alexandrovich is the son of Alexander.

A daughter adds -ovna to the father's name and so Marya Ivanovna is the daughter of Ivan.

What would your name be in Russian?

First write down your name. _____

Next write down your father's last name. _____

If you are a boy add -vich to it. _____

If you are a girl add -ovna to it. _____

Write down what you would be called in Russia. _____

Now think about names in general. Many common names have nicknames. For instance, Robert might be called Bob or Robbie, while Suzanne might be called Sue or Susie.

Choose a girl's name and a boy's name. Write them down here and on the lines underneath write some of the nicknames for each.

Girl's Name	**Boy's Name**
_____	_____
_____	_____
_____	_____
_____	_____

Can you think of any other names that have nicknames. Write some more down here. Are there common endings to the names?

_____

_____

_____

After you have written down some of the nicknames, study them. Do you see a pattern emerging from the names themselves?

Famous Russians

Russia is a country with a broad and varied background. It has produced names that are part of history, both past and present. These have included contributions in the fields of literature, the arts, politics, and science, to name but a few.

Activity

Choose one of the names below and do some research on this famous person. Write a report about him or her. Make sure in your report that you include a brief background about the person, the role this person has played in Russian history, and the changes that came about because of this person's involvement.

- Anastasia
- Catherine I (Catherine the Great)
- Anton Chekhov
- Sergei Diaghilev
- Michel Fokine
- Yuri Gagarin
- Mikhail S. Gorbachev
- Ivan IV (Ivan the Terrible)
- Alexei Kosygin
- Nikita S. Khrushchev
- V. I. Lenin
- Nicholas II
- Vaslav Nijinsky

- Boris Pasternak
- Ivan Pavlov
- Anna Pavlova
- Peter I (Peter the Great)
- Alexander S. Pushkin
- Alexander Solzhenitsyn
- Joseph Stalin
- Alex Tolstoy
- Leo Tolstoy
- Valentina Tershkova
- Leon Trotsky
- Boris N. Yeltsin

The Nutcracker

The Nutcracker ballet was written by Peter Ilich Tchaikovsky in 1892. He was a Russian composer who lived between 1840 and 1893. Tchaikovsky was the first Russian composer whose music was included in standard western musical programs. His music is richly melodical and memorable lyric.

His music included symphonies and concertos among, them the "Manfred Symphony," "Piano Concerto No. 1 in B-flat major," and "Serenade for Strings." He also wrote three ballets, *Swan Lake* in 1877, *The Sleeping Beauty* in 1890, and *The Nutcracker* in 1882. These ballets are all popular. They are often performed today.

The story of *The Nutcracker* is often performed around Christmas time. In the story, a little girl named Maria receives a nutcracker as a Christmas gift from her godfather, Dr. Drosselmayer. Her brother, Fritz, breaks it. The nutcracker is repaired and magically comes to life, leading the toys in battle against the mice. Later, he takes Maria to The Land of Sweets.

Activity

Begin this activity by listening to a recording of *The Nutcracker Suite* by Tchaikovsky. *(RCA Classics for Kids,* 1993, contains one recording.) As you listen to the music, try one of the activities listed below.

1. Bring in a standard nutcracker and various types of nuts. Crack some of them. Describe the mechanism of a nutcracker. What type of simple machine is the nutcracker? Did you place all the nuts in the same place to crack them? What were the differences in the nuts?

2. Bring a nutcraker of the type in *The Nutcracker* ballet.

3. Design a fancy nutcracker. Consider how it will work. Use another sheet of paper to sketch out what your nutcracker will look like. Challenge: Use the sketch of your nutcracker and make a 3-dimensional model of one. Use your creativity and imagination to create the nutcracker.

A Space Mission

The year 1957 is credited as the start of the space age. It was in that year that Russia launched the first satellite to circle the earth. This craft was ball-shaped, weighed about 183 pounds (77 kg) and was 22 inches (56 cm) across. This amazing flying machine was called *Sputnik*. It was soon followed by *Sputnik II* which carried the first dog in space, an animal named Laika.

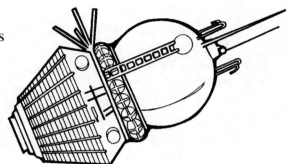

On April 21, 1961, Russia launched its first spacecraft carrying cosmonauts—a word coined from two Greek words that mean sailor of the universe. The first cosmonaut was Yuri Gagarin, who travelled on the spaceship *Vostok*.

Through the years, the United States and Russia have worked together to further space exploration. For this activity, plan a joint mission in space between the two countries.

Activity

1. Form two teams to work together. Begin by building a space ship out of a refrigerator or other large appliance boxes. Create both an outside and an inside. Include any necessary instruments or paint an instrument panel for the inside. Name the spaceship.

2. Do some astronaut training. Try some of the experiments below.

   a. Does practice improve reaction time? Use a yard or meter stick and try to catch it between your thumb and finger. Time each try. Do they improve?

   b. How fast do some muscles tire out? Use a hardcover book lifted to shoulder height. At what point do you begin to feel the lifting? How many times do you have to repeat the exercise?

   c. How does exercise affect heart rate? Take your pulse for one minute. Then do some exercises such as jumping or running for five minutes. Take your pulse again and compare the rates.

3. What are the duties of an astronaut or cosmonaut? Do some research and list them. Then share what you have learned with your team.

_____

_____

_____

_____

_____

_____

France

1. **Map of France,** page 83

   Discuss the country's location, borders, geographical features, climate, and cities.

   Extending Activities:

   Assign group reports on the following topics:

   - Geographical diversity.
   - Rich farmland. (France is Western Europe's leading agricultural country.)

2. **Facts About France; French Words and Phrases,** page 84

   Have students color the flag.

   Assign reports as suggested on page 4.

   Practice saying the French words and phrases. Ask students to use them in sentences.

3. **Landmarks of Paris,** page 85

   Extending Activities:

   - Show pictures of French castles. Draw a floor plan of a typical castle. Build a model of a castle.
   - Have students draw pictures or make models of their favorite landmarks of Paris.
   - Have students act as tour guides of their favorite landmarks. They should describe the history and point out the special features of the landmarks.

4. **View Art at the Louvre in Paris,** page 86

   Extending Activities:

   - Show pictures of paintings by Monet, Cezanne, and Renoir. Display several in your classroom.
   - Show pictures of paintings of other French artists.
   - Discuss the style of the Impressionists. Compare it with other styles of painting.

5. **Visit the Curie Institute in Paris,** page 87

   Extending Activities:

   - Discuss the history and significance of Nobel Prizes.
   - Research the life and accomplishments of Marie Curie.
   - Discuss the difference between chemistry and physics.

6. **Ride in the Tour de France,** page 88

   Make a copy of the map on page 83 for each student.

Extending Activities:

- Instead of allowing students to choose cities along their Tour de France routes, assign cities and other sites to avoid duplication. Ask each student to give an oral report so the class is exposed to information about all of France.
- Discuss preparation for participating in the Tour de France. What physical training would be necessary? What should a cyclist take on the trip?
- Discuss bicycle safety.

7. **Travel Down the Loire River.**

   - Show pictures of the countryside along the Loire River. Discuss the kinds of crops grown.
   - Study the types of soil that make good farmland. Do experiments comparing plants grown in different types of soil.
   - Show pictures of French castles. Draw a floor plan of a typical castle. Build a model of a castle.
   - Discuss safety, comfort, and the daily lifestyle of people who lived in the castles.

8. **Stop for a Picnic.**

   - Taste French bread, several French cheeses, and fruit. Discuss the daily eating habits of people in France.
   - Discuss fine French cuisine.
   - Study wine production in France.

9. **Visit Lascaux Cave.**

   - Show pictures of the prehistoric paintings.
   - Discuss the possible motives of people who painted the prehistoric art.
   - Ask students to draw their own cave art. Discuss what tools people of that time period had available to use.

Bibliography

Fiction

Bernelmans, Ludwig. *Madeline.* (Puffin, 1977)

Galdone, Paul. *Puss in Boots.* (Clarion, 1983)

Perrault, Charles. *Cinderella.* (Dial, 1985)

Map of France

Paris

Facts About France

Capital:	Paris
Largest city:	Paris
Language:	French
Currency:	Franc
Population:	59,551,000
Area:	210,026 sq. mi. (543,965 sq. km)
Agriculture:	Livestock, barley, com, oats, sugar beets, vegetables, fruits, flowers, flax
Industries:	Aircraft, automobiles, machinery, chemicals, iron, steel, clothing, perfume, food processing, wine, tourism, mining, fishing
Flag Colors:	Left—blue, Center—white, Right—red

French Words and Phrases

Bonjour	Good morning; good day; a common greeting
Au revoir	Goodbye
Slil vous plait	Please
Merci	Thank you
Comment allez-vous?	How are you?
Je vais bien	I am well.
L'ecole	School
La classe	Class
Les livres	Books
Le crayon	Pencil
La table	Table
Le chaise	Chair
Le cafe	Coffee
Le lait	Milk
Le pain	Bread
Le poisson	Fish
Le poulet	Chicken

Add three words or phrases that you want to learn in French:

_____

_____

_____

Landmarks of Paris

Welcome to Paris! This is not only the capital of France; it is the country's heart. It is the center of industry, government, finance, education, culture, and the arts.

Paris is a beautiful city with a rich history. It is called the City of Light. It has many gardens, parks, and avenues that are lined with trees.

Pictured below are three of the most famous landmarks of Paris. Choose one and find out more about it.

Where is it? _____

When was it built? _____

Why was it built? _____

Who was in charge of building it? _____

What is special about it? _____

How is it used today? _____

View Art at the Louvre in Paris

The Louvre is one of the largest and most famous art museums in the world. It contains more than a million works of art!

Some of the paintings in the Louvre are the work of the French artists Monet, Cezanne, and Renoir. In 1874, a group of painters, including these three artists, held an exhibit of their works. Their paintings were done in a new style and received much negative criticism. Instead of copying a scene exactly, they painted their impression of it. They used light and color in new ways. These artists were known as *Impressionists*. This name was based on the painting called *Impression, Sunrise* by Monet.

Find out more about each of these painters. Then choose one painting and create a copy of it on a separate sheet of paper.

Claude Monet

When did he live? _____

Give one interesting fact about his life. _____

What subjects did he use most? _____

Name three of his paintings. _____

What do you like or dislike about his paintings? _____

Paul Cezanne

When did he live? _____

Give one interesting fact about his life. _____

What subjects did he use most? _____

Name three of his paintings. _____

What do you like or dislike about his paintings? _____

Auguste Renoir

When did he live? _____

Give one interesting fact about his life. _____

What subjects did he use most? _____

Name three of his paintings. _____

What do you like or dislike about his paintings? _____

Visit the Curie Institute in Paris

Marie Curie was a scientist who worked in Paris. She was awarded the Nobel Prize for physics in 1903. She was awarded the Nobel Prize for chemistry in 1911.

In the following experiment, you will mix ingredients and experience a physical change in matter. Think of Marie Curie as you enjoy your lesson in chemistry and physics.

The matter around us exists in three forms: solid, liquid, and gas. Water, for example, is ice as a solid, water as a liquid, and steam as a gas. Matter can be made to change state by heating or by cooling because energy is added to or taken away from it. You can identify the state of matter as follows:

Solid — definite shape, definite volume

Liquid — no definite shape, definite volume

Gas — no definite shape, no definite volume

Here is a delicious way to change matter from one state to another. You will need to work in a small group to complete the following activity.

Materials: one three-pound (1.35 kg) coffee can and lid; one one-pound (.45 kg) coffee can and lid; crushed ice; rock salt; masking tape; small paper cups and spoons; wire whisk

Ingredients: one cup (250 mL) whipping cream

one cup (250 mL) milk

½ cup (125 mL) sugar

½ teaspoon (2.5 mL) vanilla

Directions:

Following the steps below to make your special treat ice cream! Think about the changes in the states of matter that occur as you prepare the ice cream. Be ready to discuss the questions below among the members of your group.

1. Mix the ice cream ingredients in the one-pound (.45 kg) coffee can. Securely tape the lid on the one-pound coffee can.

2. Put a thin layer of crushed ice on the bottom of the three-pound (1.35 kg) coffee can and sprinkle rock salt over the ice.

3. Place the one-pound can inside the three-pound can. Pack layers of ice and rock salt around the smaller can until the larger can is full. Put the lid on the larger can and seal it with tape.

4. Find a space on the floor where you and your partner can sit five feet (about 2 meters) apart. Choose an area that can be easily cleaned in case of leakage. Roll the coffee can back and forth for 15 minutes. Check to see if the ice cream has formed by taking the one-pound can out and shaking it. If there is not sloshing, the ice cream is done. Spoon the ice cream into cups and enjoy it.

Questions for Discussion:

- Was the ice cream mixture solid, liquid, or gas before rolling? Explain your answer.
- Was the mixture solid, liquid, or gas after rolling? Explain your answer.

Ride in the Tour de France

Every summer, more than 100 professional cyclists ride in the Tour de France. They ride every day for nearly a month. They travel all over the country and finish in Paris.

Imagine that you are in charge of the race. On a map of France, draw the route you would plan for the cyclists. On the lines below, list the mountains, rivers, bodies of water, and cities the cyclists will see. (Remember that the race must end in Paris.)

_____

_____

_____

_____

_____

_____

_____

_____

_____

Choose one of the cities on your list. _____

Explain why you included it on your Tour de France. _____

_____

Find out more about the city and answer the following questions.

How large is it? _____

What is the history of the city? _____

_____

What industries are located in the city? _____

_____

What is special about the city? _____

_____

Italy

1. **Map of Italy,** page 90

   Discuss the country's location, borders, geographical features, climate, and cities.

   Extending Activities:

   Assign group reports on the following topics:

   - Geographical diversity, ranging from southern seashore to northern Alps
   - Italian opera
   - Automobile design and production

2. **Facts About Italy; Italian Words and Phrases,** page 91

   Have students color the flag.

   Assign reports as suggested on page 4.

   Practice saying the Italian words and phrases. Ask students to use them in sentences.

3. **The City of Rome,** page 92

   Extending Activities:

   - Research the Roman arch and construct a model from clay or sugar cubes.
   - Research Roman fountains; bring in pictures and discuss.

4. **Rome Quotation Search,** page 93

   A. La Fontaine (Fables)

   B. St. Augustine

   C. Juvenal

   D. R. Kipling

   E. Shakespeare (Julius Caesar)

   F. E. A. Poe (To Helen)

   G. St. Augustine

   H. Cicero

   I. Cervantes (Don Quixote)

   J. Caesar Augustus

   Extending Activities:

   - Find out more about famous Romans.

5. **The City of Naples,** pages 94-95

   Extending Activities:

   - Write a story, "I survived the eruption of Mt. Vesuvius." Include how you escaped and what you saw.
   - With two other students, prepare a TV newscast covering the destruction of Pompeii. One student is the anchor, the other two are reporters who will broadcast from different parts of the city. Be sure to write a script with dialogue for each newscaster.

6. **The City of Florence,** page 96

   Extending Activities:

   - Write a dialogue and perform a scene of the great Florentine art patron, Lorenzo de Medici, welcoming the following artists to Florence: Michelangelo, Leonardo da Vinci, Benvenuto Cellini, Petrarch, and Dante. Have him praise them for some specific work they have created or written. Have him ask each what he would like to work on now. Have the artists respond, mentioning actual works that still exist. Have Lorenzo praise them again and grant them specific salaries, places to live, allowances for expenses for their materials, etc., while they live in Florence.

7. **The City of Pisa,** page 97

   Extending Activity:

   - Write a report about Galileo's famous experiment from The Leaning Tower of Pisa. Draw a diagram illustrating it.
   - The Italian government once offered a prize for the best solution to stop the tower from continuing its slow tilting. Research the ways that modern buildings' foundations are made. Prepare some careful diagrams to show how we try to build solid foundations for tall buildings today.

8. **Food of Italy,** page 98

   Extending Activities:

   - Visit an Italian restaurant.

Bibliography for Italy

Nonfiction

Volcanoes

Lauber, Patricia. *Volcano.* (Bradbury, 1986)

Map of Italy

Rome

Facts About Italy

Capital:	Rome
Largest city:	Rome
Language:	Italian
Currency:	Lira
Population:	57,679,000
Area:	116,320 sq. mi. (301,268 sq. km)
Agriculture:	Fruit, vegetables, grains, livestock, olives
Industry:	Clothing, shoes, machinery, motor vehicles, petroleum products
Flag colors:	Left—green, Center—white, Right—red

Italian Words and Phrases

Buona sera	Good evening
Buon giorno	Good day
Arrivederci	Goodbye
Grazie	Thank you
Per favore	Please
Ragazzo	Boy
Ragazza	Girl
Padre	Father
Madre	Mother
Fratello	Brother
Sorella	Sister
Casa	House
Scarpe	Shoes
Strada	Street
Tavola	Table
Acqua	Water
Verdure	Vegetables

Add three words or phrases that you want to learn in Italian:

_____

_____

_____

Rome (Roma)

Your visit to Italy begins in Rome, called The Eternal City because of its long history. It is the capital of Italy and has been an important center of civilization for over 2,000 years. Amid modem buildings of steel and glass, great monuments and structures from ages past still stand. The beauty of past and present combine here to remind us of the greatness of this city that once ruled the Western World for hundreds of years. That ancient time, that vast area, those mighty people of yesterday—all that is what comes to mind when we refer to The Roman Empire. The language, literature, architecture, and government of today's world have all been strongly shaped by this one city and its people. Rome is located about ten miles (16 km) inland on the banks of the Tiber River. The ancient city was built on seven hills east of the river but now extends much farther, of course. In ancient days, all the streets spread out from the Capitoline, the heart of the city then. Before we set out to explore the city, take a look at the map of the ancient city below. Then locate the following structures and streets on your own blank map of Rome. Label them neatly and color each hill district a separate color. Label all streets.

Map of Old Rome

1. The Seven Hills
2. Trajan's Column
3. The Colosseum
4. The Pantheon
5. The Arch of Constantine
6. Circus Maximus
7. The Baths of Trajan
8. The Forum of Julius Caesar
9. The Roman Forum
10. The Catacombs of Sant'Agnese

Now that you have familiarized yourselves with map of the old city, and some of its major monuments, you will visit a museum of Roman history and research some aspects of ancient Roman life. Select from one of the topics to make your group or individual reports. Be sure to make a careful drawing or model to illustrate your research. Share this with the class.

1. Colosseum
2. Pantheon
3. Bath Houses
4. Chariot Races
5. Catacombs
6. Arches and Aqueducts
7. Romulus and Remus
8. Gladiators

Rome Quotation Search

This city is so famous that our language is filled with references to it, even today. Some of these references are quotations from famous authors, but they have become a common part of our culture.

See if you can locate the meaning and source of each of the following expressions. You may use your reference library or ask your friends and relatives for help.

1. *All roads lead to Rome.*

   Source: _____   Meaning: _____

2. *When in Rome, do as the Romans.*

   Source: _____   Meaning: _____

3. *Everything in Rome is expensive.*

   Source: _____   Meaning: _____

4. *Rome is above the nations.*

   Source: _____   Meaning: _____

5. *This was the noblest Roman of them all.*

   Source: _____   Meaning: _____

6. *. . . the glory that was Greece and the grandeur that was Rome.*

   Source: _____   Meaning: _____

7. *Rome has spoken; the case is closed.*

   Source: _____   Meaning: _____

8. *I am a Roman citizen.*

   Source: _____   Meaning: _____

9. *Rome wasn't built in a day.*

   Source: _____   Meaning: _____

10. *I found Rome bricks and left it marble.*

   Source: _____   Meaning: _____

Naples (Napoli)

Leaving Rome, you will travel south to Naples, located on a large bay overlooked by one of the most famous landmarks of the world—Mt. Vesuvius, at 4,190 ft. (1277 km) high, is still a dangerous volcano. Towering over the city seven miles (11 km) to the north, this volcano is most famous for what happened on August 24 in the year 79. Vesuvius erupted violently, completely covering the towns of Pompeii and Herculaneum. The inhabitants were trapped and killed, covered in ash and mudflow from 20 (6 m) to 60 (18 m) feet deep. Seventeen hundred years later, the towns were uncovered and found to be in an amazing state of preservation. Shops were filled with goods, food was found in ovens, bodies of pets and people were found in the positions they held when overcome by the explosion. You may walk the streets of these towns today and see for yourself what they looked like almost 2000 years ago. Meanwhile, Vesuvius still spews columns of steam and cinders from time to time, and farmers still work the rich lower slopes around the mountain.

Activities

1. Research the ancient Roman myth of Vulcan, god of fire. Prepare a report to the class telling of Vulcan's adventures, his achievements, his appearance, and his marriage.

2. Research the basic types, causes, and actions of volcanoes. Be sure to include drawings showing the inner workings of the volcano and its eruption. Present and explain your research to the class in a notebook and oral report.

3. Draw a map showing major areas of volcanic activity in the world. Make this on a large sheet of chart paper that can be posted on the classroom wall.

4. Provide a key for names and locations of major volcanoes of the world and then place small silver, red, and gold stars in appropriate places on your classroom globe. Use the different colors to represent active, intermittent, and dormant volcanoes.

5. Write a report about the destruction of Pompeii and Herculaneum.

6. Compare the eruption of Mt. St. Helens to that of Vesuvius. Use drawings to illustrate. Explain this to the class.

7. Provide your own drawings to illustrate, label, and explain the following terms as they are used with volcanoes.

A. magma	F. crater	K. dormant
B. lava	G. crust	L. extinct
C. eruption	H. mantle	M. intermittent
D. central vent	I. outer core	N. active
E. side vent	J. inner core	

Naples *(cont.)*

Experiments

---

1. Build a volcano. Give each student a marble-sized ball of clay and a cone-shaped cup. Have the students place their names on the cups. Place the ball of clay inside the point of the cup. Mix plaster of Paris—about 8 lb. (3.6 kg) for a class of 30—a little bit at a time to the consistency of thick pancake batter. Put the mix into the cups and let set for 24 hours. Then give the students their volcanoes and several sheets of newspaper. Have them peel away the cup and remove the clay ball. They should have a volcano with a crater. Stand the volcano upright on the spread-out newspaper. Prepare the volcano for an eruption. Place about one teaspoon (5 mL) of baking soda into the "crater" which has been lined with plastic wrap. Mix red and yellow food coloring with ½ teaspoon (2.5 mL) of white vinegar in a separate cup. Pour the vinegar slowly into the baking soda. Observe what happens.

2. Make a volcano. This demonstration will help to show how heated liquid tends to rise within the volcano. The materials necessary are a small drinking glass, a small bottle with a neck opening smaller than the drinking glass, a piece of cardboard larger then the drinking glass opening, a pin, water, and food coloring.

   A. Poke a small hole in the cardboard with the pin.

   B. Half-fill the glass with cold water.

   C. Put four or five drops of food coloring into the bottle and fill with hot water from the tap.

   D. Place the cardboard over the top of the glass and hold it firmly in place. Quickly turn the glass upside down (still holding the cardboard in place). Now place the cardboard and glass on top of the bottle. Be sure the pin hole is centered over the bottle opening. The water will not fall out as long as you keep the cardboard firmly over the top of the glass. If it does spill, simply refill and start over.

   E. Still holding the cardboard, press down gently on the glass. Puffs of color should rise through the pin hole into the glass above. (Since warm water is lighter than cold water, it rises).

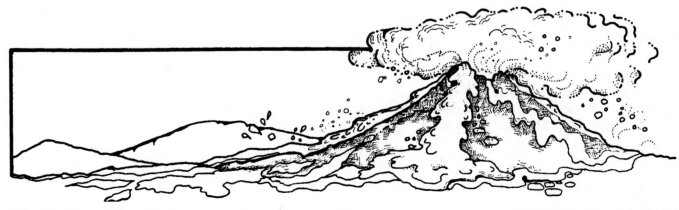

Florence (Firenze)

We travel north from Naples past Rome and up the "boot" of Italy to reach this city. Well over a thousand years after the height of ancient Rome, Florence became world famous as a center for the arts, especially sculpture, painting, and literature. Today, it spreads across both banks of the Amo River at the base of the Apennine Mountains. The modem Italian language owes much to the dialect that was developed in this city during the Middle Ages. Between the years of 1300 and 1600, Florence achieved great power. It was a period of time we now call the Renaissance or "rebirth." We call it that because it almost seemed as if the great achievements of ancient Rome were being born again, many of them taking place right here in Florence. A powerful family named the Medici governed the city, attracting writers, painters, and sculptors to live and work there. They paid them well and sponsored their works. You may recognize two of the most famous artists—Michelangelo and Leonardo da Vinci.

Our first visit will be to the square in the center of the city—Piazza della Signoria. Then we will enjoy seeing all the works in the following galleries: Uffizi Palace, National Museum of Bargello, and the Galleria dell'Accademia where Michelangelo's statue of David stands.

Activities

A. Individually or in groups, research and write reports on any of the following writers, artists, or painters. You may include a copy of your own favorite art work if you wish.

1. Leonardo da Vinci
2. Fra Angelico
3. Giotto
4. Michelangelo
5. Giovanni Boccaccio
6. Dante
7. Petrarch
8. Niccolo Machiavelli
9. Raphael
10. Benvenuto Cellini

B. Bring in pictures, slides, films, or videotapes showing some of the works still on display in Florence. Discuss.

C. Read the story of "Pinocchio."

1. In small groups, write dialogue for a puppet play about the story. Bind the script in a folder with an illustrated title page.

2. Create puppets (marionettes) for characters to enact the play.

3. Present the play for an audience.

Pisa

Leaving Florence, we will travel west to the town of Pisa near the west coast of Italy. Here stands one of the most famous buildings in the world. The Leaning Tower of Pisa is one of three church buildings, all parts of the Cathedral of Pisa. The tower was built to house the church bells and is called a campanile. It is 180 feet (55 m) tall and has walls that are 13 feet (4 m) thick at the bottom and about 6 feet (2 m) thick at the top. The bottom story has 15 arches, while each of the next six stories has 30 arches. The very top story holds the bells and has 12 arches. If you walk to the very top, you will climb almost 300 steps. The building was started in the year 1173 and finished about 700 years ago. The foundation was built on unstable soil, a mixture of sand, clay, and water. As a result, it began tipping to one side, and today it leans over about 14 and ½ feet (4.4 m). (The famous scientist Galileo, who was born here, used the tower to drop weights and measure the speed of falling objects.) The tower has continued to tip at a rate of about an inch (2.5 cm) every nine years. Just recently, Italy has announced that engineers have succeeded in stabilizing this movement by shoring up the foundation soil. If the leaning continued, of course, this great architectural treasure of the past would eventually

Activities

fall.

1. **Build a Soap Model:** Build a soap carving model of the eight-story Leaning Tower of Pisa. Each story should be a separate cylinder of soap. Carve the base first. The next story should be a bit smaller. When it is completed, dampen the bottom and stick it to the top of the first story. Continue until all stories are completed. If done as a small-group activity, each person would be responsible for one or two stories. Use paper clips as carving tools to score the arches around each story. When the tower is completed, it may be placed on a base of sand that will allow it to be tipped slightly, just like the original. Modeling clay can be substituted for soap if desired.

2. **Tower-Building Contest (newspaper):** Using teamwork and critical thinking skills, have partners see who can build the tallest free-standing tower with two full pages of newspaper and masking tape. The tower must be able to stand alone. Structures built from rolled newspaper can be surprisingly strong. Scissors, newspaper, and masking tape are the only materials allowed in this contest!

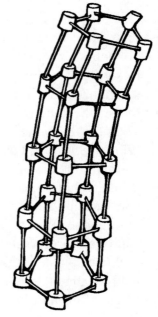

3. **Tower-Building Contest (toothpicks):** Again using teamwork and critical thinking skills, have partners see who can build the highest free-standing toothpick tower, using glue or small marshmallows to connect the toothpicks. Encourage students to use as many geometric shapes as possible in designing their towers. Have them identify and count the number of squares, triangles, sides, angles, etc., in the completed tower. Prepare a fact card containing this information plus other interesting measurements to accompany each tower. The base size for all towers should be the same—about 6 inches (15 cm).

Food of Italy

It would not be right to leave Italy without sampling some of the especially tasty foods for which this country is famous all around the world. Of course, we are talking about pasta!

"Pasta" is an Italian word meaning dough. The best pasta is made from milled hard-grain wheat, often mixed with water, seasoning, and flour, It is cut into many different shapes and dried. There is an almost endless variety of ribbons, strings, tubes, spirals, shells, and stars sold in the stores of the world today. They are all known as pasta, and each has its own special name—most of them Italian. All of them are rich in carbohydrates, some have been enriched with vitamins and other nutrients, and some have been mixed with spinach for a green color. This very versatile food is usually boiled until soft and slightly chewy. Then it is mixed with tomato sauce, meat, cheese, vegetables, and sauces in various combinations. The results have become favorite dishes of people all over the world.

Prepare a pasta poster with four main headings: Strings, Tubes, Flat Ribbons, and Special Shapes. See how many different shapes and sizes of pasta you can collect in class. Glue a sample of each type on a line under the appropriate column. Carefully print the proper name under each sample. Examples: spaghetti, macaroni, fettuccine, rigatoni, ravioli, canneloni, tortellini, vermicelli, linguini, lasagna noodles, etc. At the bottom of the chart, place a heading for nutrients. List the vitamins, minerals, and other nutrients that appear on the packages containing the various pastas on your Pasta Poster.

Open an Italian Restaurant!

Your first job, of course, is to decide what you will prepare.
- With a partner, collect some sample menus from Italian restaurants as a start. Also, check with your parents and a cookbook or two for favorite Italian dishes and recipes.
- Prepare a list of exactly what dishes you will serve. Include salads, soups, appetizers, main courses, desserts, and beverages. You are ready to produce an appetizing menu for your restaurant.
- Next, prepare a menu using scissors, colored markers and pens; tagboard or other sturdy paper, paper fasteners, and colored yarn.
- First decide how large your menu should be. Some restaurants provide quite large ones, about 10 inches (25 cm) by 15 inches (38 cm).
- Design a cover with your restaurant's name on it. You may include a cover picture that symbolizes something from Italy—a Roman fountain, Mt. Vesuvius, a gondola, etc.
- Make a heading on separate pages for each of the types of foods listed in number two above. Then list the names of the different soups, main courses, etc., that you are serving. Be sure to print carefully and use the correct Italian names. Decide on a price for each item and place it on the right side of the menu.
- When all your pages are completed, bind your menu together with the cover sheet on top. You may punch holes in the left hand margins and use paper fasteners or colorful yarn to thread through the holes so your menu will open easily. What do you think would be the most appropriate colors to use? (Hint: What are the colors in the Italian flag?)

A successful conclusion to this activity, naturally, is to have a pizza party while each group passes its menu around for the others to read. (Otherwise, everyone might die of hunger!) To aid the digestion, listen to a tape of Pavarotti or some other artist singing Italian arias.

Greece

1. **Map of Greece,** page 101

   Discuss the country's location, borders, geographical features, climate, and cities.

   Extending Activities:

   Assign group reports on the following topics:

   - Geographical diversity, ranging from seacoasts to rocky slopes and mountains.
   - Islands
   - Mediterranean climate

2. **Facts about Greece; Greek Words and Phrases,** page 102

   Have students color the flag.

   Assign reports as suggested on page 4.

   Practice saying the Greek words and phrases. Ask students to use them in sentences.

3. **The Greek Alphabet,** page 103

   Extending activities:

   - Study words with Greek roots, suffixes, prefixes.
   - Bring in books, magazines, newspapers, written in Greek.
   - Mount Greek travel posters in room.
   - Invite a native speaker of Greek to read orally for accurate pronunciation.
   - Research early Phoenician letter forms and their relation to the Greek alphabet.
   - Make comparison charts of Phoenician, Greek, and Roman letter forms. Post in room.

4. **Boustrophedon,** page 104

   Extending Activities:

   - Investigate how other languages are written.
   - Try writing some letters on paper and showing them in the mirror. What happens to them?

5. **Aesop's Fables,** page 105

   Extending Activities:

   - Discuss sources of Aesop's fables—India, Far East.
   - Discuss major characteristic of fables—talking animals, moral lesson, brevity, etc.
   - Examine fables of other countries—e.g., India, Africa, Australia, Northern Europe.
   - Assign oral reports telling fables as simple stories. At the conclusion of each, ask the class to supply the moral.
   - Compare La Fontaine's Fables with those of Aesop.
   - Discuss differences between fairy tales and fables.
   - Read Greek myths and early stories: " Jason and the Argonauts," "Perseus and Medusa," "The Labors of Heracles," "Tales of the Titans," etc.
   - Draw pictures of mythological creatures minotaur, centaur, etc.
   - Discuss the differences and similarities between myths and fables. Note the rich imagination of the Greeks in leaving us this store of literary fantasy.
   - Bring in diagrams and pictures of constellations. Discuss the mythological background for their names—Orion, Pegasus, Cassiopeia, Gemini, etc.
   - Compare Roman names of planets to Greek names for the same figures—Mars and Ares, Venus and Aphrodite, Jupiter and Zeus. Discuss and make charts for the Greek Gods who were adopted by the Romans and given Roman names.

Greece (cont.)

6. **Greek Measurement,** page 106

   Extending Activities:

   • Research early Greek mathematics.
   • Learn words for Greek numbers from one to ten.
   • Read the story of Pythagoras.
   • Discuss geometry—"earth measurement" literally in Greek.
   • Try some simple geometric constructions— squares, triangles, circles, rectangles.
   • Follow up the constructions with measurement.
   • Illustrate, explain, construct right angles.

7. **Olympic Games,** page 107

   Scavenger Hunt Answers:

   1. 776 B.C.
   2. Discus, javelin, long jump, sprint, wrestling
   3. Every 4 years
   4. Three interlocking circles over two interlocking circles
   5. The Battle of Marathon in 490 B.C. Pheidippides ran from the plain of Marathon to Athens to tell the people of their victory over the Persians.
   6. Third place
   7. Mark Spitz—swimming
   8. Chariot races
   9. Greece
   10. Jennifer Capriati
   11. Sabre, epee, foil
   12. Each member receives a medal.
   13. Free style and Greco-Roman style
   14. Rowing
   15. Horseback riding
   16. Germany
   17. Unified Tem (the former U.S.S.R. team)
   18. 43.5 seconds—Quincy Watts of the U.S.A.
   19. 294 ft. 2 in. (89.66 m)—Jan Zelezny of Czechoslovakia
   20. 24.79 seconds—Yan Wenyi of China

Extending Activities:

• In small groups, research the history of the original Olympic games in Greece.
• In small groups, research the history of the modem Olympic games since 1896.
• Write reports on some of the ancient sports such as chariot racing.
• Hold discussions on whether students think the modern game of table tennis should be included in the Olympics. If so, why not golf? Make lists of sports not included that you think should be.

Bibliography

Aesop's Fables. (Avenel Books, Facsimile of the 1912 edition, 1988)

Descamps-Lequime, Sophie and Denise Vernerey. *Ancient Greeks: In the Land of Gods.* (Millbrook Pr., 1992)

Pearson, Anne. *Ancient Greece.* (Eyewitness Book). (Alfred A. Knopf, 1992)

Map of Greece

Athens

Facts About Greece

Capital:	Athens
Largest city:	Athens
Language:	Greek
Currency:	Drachma
Population:	10,623,000
Area:	50,962 sq. mi. (131,990 sq. km)
Agriculture:	Wheat, com, grapes, olives, livestock
Industry:	Cement, chemicals, textiles, clothing, mining, shipping
Flag colors:	White cross in blue field, stripes alternate blue and white starting with blue at the top

Greek Words and Phrases

The English alphabet is derived from that of the Greeks, but it is not identical. Moreover, pronunciations are not the same. Therefore, these first words will appear spelled in English to approximate their Greek pronunciations.

Biblion	Book
Pateras	Father
Skholio	School
Pena	Pen
Trapezi	Table
Mitera	Mother
Stoma	Mouth
Nero	Water
Ne	Yes
Ohi	No
Zestos	Hot
Kalo	Good
Sighnomi	Sorry
Pino	I'm hungry.
Dhipso	I'm thirsty.
Ghia sas	Hello
Entaxi	That's fine.

Add three words and phrases that you want to learn in Greek.

_____

_____

_____

The Greek Alphabet

The Greek alphabet was developed from an earlier form begun by the Phoenician people. Our present English alphabet is in turn developed from the Greek one. In fact, the name alphabet comes from the names of the first two Greek letters—Alpha and Beta. Below is a copy of the Greek alphabet (with only 24 letters) and the names for each letter. See if you can write some English words using the equivalent Greek letters.

Alpha	å	A	Nu	ν	N
Beta	ß	B	Xi	ξ	Ξ
Gamma	γ	Γ	Omicron	o	O
Delta	∂	Δ	Pi	π	Π
Epsilon	ε	E	Rho	p	P
Zeta	ζ	Z	Sigma	σ, s	Σ
Eta	η	H	Tau	τ	T
Theta	θ	Θ	Upsilon	υ	Y
Iota	ι	I	Phi	φ	Φ
Kappa	κ	K	Chi	χ	X
Lambda	λ	Λ	Psi	ψ	Ψ
Mu	μ	M	Omega	ω	Ω

_____

_____

_____

_____

_____

_____

_____

_____

_____

Boustrophedon

Not every culture has chosen to write their language across the page as this writing appears. Some cultures place their script up and down, or vertically, on the page and then read it from right to left. At one stage in the development of Greece, the people experimented with a writing form they called *boustrophedon*. The words started on the top right hand side of the page and moved to the left. When they reached the end of the line, they continued to the next lower line and wrote from left to right, just as we do today. At the end of that line, they would drop to the next line and again write from right to left. Thus the writing would continue, zigzagging to the bottom of the page.

On the following lines, see if you can write the second, third fourth, and fifth sentences of the paragraph above in boustrophedon form. The first sentence appears below as an example for you.

Example: ·

the across language their write to chosen has culture every Not

page as this writing appears. Some cultures place their . . . .

(Eventually, the Greeks abandoned the boustrophedon format about 500 B.C. and started writing about 500 B.C. and started writing from left to right on every line.)

_____

_____

_____

_____

_____

_____

_____

_____

_____

_____

_____

_____

Aesop's Fables

One of the best known literary collections we have of early Greek origin is *Aesop's Fables*. A somewhat shadowy figure, Aesop was supposedly a clever slave who did not actually author his stories but did make a fine collection of known fables. The following sixteen fables may be read orally to the class with a discussion of the lesson or moral to take place following each tale. Read three or four fables a day until all sixteen are completed. It might be helpful to keep a record on the board or chart paper of each title to aid in review and memory.

1. **The Fox and the Grapes**—(Sour grapes: We belittle what we cannot have.)
2. **The Goose that Laid the Golden Egg**—(The greedy want more and often lose all.)
3. **The Fox and the Crow** (Some people do foolish things when flattered.)
4. **The Spendthrift and the Swallow**—(One swallow does not make a summer.)
5. **The Lion and the Mouse**—(Even the weak can help the strong.)
6. **The Crow and the Pitcher**—(Necessity is the mother of invention.)
7. **The Wolf in Sheep's Clothing** (If you pretend to be someone else, you may receive that person's fate.)
8. **The Milkmaid and Her Pail**—(Don't count your chickens before they hatch.)
9. **The Bear and the Two Travelers**—(Misfortune tests the sincerity of friendship.)
10. **The Shepherd's Boy and the Wolf**—(People will not believe a liar, even when he finally tells the truth.)
11. **Fathers and Sons**—(Union is strength.)
12. **The Dog in the Manger**—(Some are so selfish they will keep others from having what they themselves cannot benefit by.)
13. **The Stag at the Pool**—(What is worth most is sometimes valued least.)
14. **Hercules and the Waggoner**—(Heaven helps those who help themselves.)
15. **The Lioness and the Vixen**—(Quality is what counts, not quantity.)
16. **The Hare and the Tortoise**—(Slow and steady wins the race of life.)

Modern Fable Writing

As we know by now, fables are brief stories that teach a moral or lesson. The characters are usually animals that talk, speaking wise or foolish lines, according to the type of creature they represent.

Often, the last line of the fable is a simple statement of the moral in a form almost like a proverb.

You are now to be a modern Aesop. Write an original fable containing animal characters. Try to choose appropriate animals for your situations. (Lions, for example, rarely appear as weak, puny figures in stories. The fox is often portrayed as shrewd and cunning.) Your story should illustrate one of the following proverbial lessons or morals. You may create a pen name for yourself from Greek myth or history if you wish—for example, you might sign your fable *Jason the Adventurous, Athena the Wise,* or *Pericles the Prudent.*

- Honesty is the best policy.
- Kindness is better than cruelty.
- Look before you leap.
- Haste makes waste.
- Three may keep a secret if two of them are dead.
- A cat in gloves catches no mice.
- You are best to yourself when you are good to others.
- Great talkers are little doers.

Early Measurement

The early Greeks used a system of measuring length based on the human body. For example, the following five units were in common use:

1. Handspan—distance from the end of the thumb to the tip of the first finger
2. Palm—length of one's palm
3. Foot length of one's foot
4. Cubit—distance from the elbow to the tip of the outstretched fingers
5. Pace—length of a single walking stride

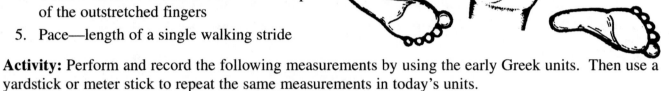

Activity: Perform and record the following measurements by using the early Greek units. Then use a yardstick or meter stick to repeat the same measurements in today's units.

	Early Greek Measure	Customary Measure	Metric Measure
Classroom width			
Classroom length			
Class door width			
Class door length			
Your height			
Friend's height			
Desk length			
Desk width			

Olympic Games

Centuries ago, the Greeks began a tradition of a love of sports, gathering together regularly for competition. The most important of those gatherings was called the Olympic Games, and we carry on that tradition today with world-wide competition. Of course, some of the games today are different from those of ancient times, but some remain virtually unchanged.

Olympic Scavenger Hunt

This is a team sport, and you are in competition with the other pairs in your class to find as many answers as you can. Your teacher will set your time limits. Otherwise, you may find your answers any way you can—from parents, friends, reference books, or personal knowledge. If you help competing teams, however, you will lower your own chances of winning.

1. What was the date of the very first Olympic Games? _____

2. What sports were in the ancient Pentathlon? _____

3. Originally, how often were the Olympic games held? _____

4. Draw the Olympic logo.

5. On what historical event is the marathon run based? _____

6. What does a bronze medal signify? _____

7. Who holds the record for the most gold medals won in one Olympics? In what events were they won?
   _____

8. Originally, what races besides foot races were held? _____

9. Which nation's athletes always enter the stadium first? _____

10. Who was the youngest female tennis medalist in 1992? _____

11. Name three separate fencing events. _____

12. Exactly how is a winning medal awarded in team sports? _____

13. Name two separate styles of wrestling. _____

14. What kind of event is single sculls? _____

15. What are equestrian events? _____

16. Which country won the most gold medals in the 1992 Winter Olympics? _____

17. Which country won the most gold medals in the 1992 Summer Olympics? _____

18. What is the Olympic record for the 400 meter men's track race? Who set that record?
    _____

19. What is the Olympic record for the javelin throw? Who set that record?
    _____

20. What is the Olympic record for the 50-meter freestyle women's swimming event? Who set that record?
    _____

United Kingdom

1. **Map of the United Kingdom,** page 109

   Discuss the country's location, borders, geographical features, climate, and cities.

   Extending Activities:

   Assign group reports on the following topics:

   - The monarchy
   - British literature
   - Colonization

2. **Facts About the United Kingdom; Words and Phrases,** page 110

   Have students color the flag.

   Assign reports as suggested on page 4.

3. **Robin Hood,** page 111

   Extending Activities:

   - Read King Arthur stories.
   - Discuss knights and their training.
   - Write a story about a knight and a dragon.
   - Make a personal coat of arms.

4. **The Game of Golf,** page 112

   Extending Activities:

   - Find out about some popular golfers and golf tournaments.
   - Do some math problems based on golf scores.

5. **London,** pages 113-114

   Extending Activities:

   - Make a travel brochure of the sights.
   - Taste English scones and tea.

6. **Find out about Stonehendge.**

   - Discuss the possible explanation for Stonehenge being there.
   - Make a model.

7. **The Loch Ness Monster**

   - Discuss the possible explanations for sighting the monster.
   - Write a story about the sighting of the monster.

8. **Visit Dublin Castle.**

   - Study the legend of the Blarney Stone.
   - Find out about leprechauns. Write a story about one.

9. **English Authors and Literature**

   There are many famous English authors. Do some research about them.

   - Read some books by British authors.
   - Discuss Shakespeare and read some plays or sonnets.
   - Share some English poetry. Chorally or dramatically read some aloud in class.

Bibliography

Nonfiction

Hill, Barbara. *Cooking the English Way.* (Lemer, 1982)

Fiction

Gannett, Ruth Stiles. *My Father's Dragon.* (Knopf, 1987)

Hodges, Margaret. *St. George and the Dragon.* Brown, 1990)

Map of United Kingdom

London

Facts About United Kingdom

Note: The United Kingdom of Great Britain is a union of four countries England, Scotland, Wales, and Northern Ireland.

Capital:	London
Largest city:	London
Language:	English
Currency:	Pound
Population:	59,647,000
Area:	94,267 sq. mi. (244,154 sq. km)
Agriculture:	Barley, livestock, wheat, sugar beets, fruits, potatoes
Industry:	Banking, metals, textiles, electronics, chemicals, oil, autos
Flag colors:	Red cross with white outline against blue background, left side of X red on the bottom of X, white on top of X; right side of X red on top of X, white on bottom of X

English Words and Phrases

biscuits	cookies
pushcar	stroller
lorry	truck
lift	elevator
bobby	police officer
petrol	gas
sweet	candy
flat	apartment
boot	car trunk
holiday	vacation

Find some more phrases and words that are used in the United Kingdom. Write them here.

_____

_____

_____

Robin Hood

The very name, Robin Hood, suggests romance and adventure. This legendary English outlaw was known to steal from the rich to give to the poor. He lived in Sherwood Forest with a band of followers known as his Merry Men. These characters included Friar Tuck who was a jolly, fat priest, and Little John who was reported to be more than 7 feet (210 cm) tall. Robin Hood also had a sweetheart called Maid Marian. Some say that Robin Hood didn't really exist; while others contend that he was a real person, Robert Fitzooth, the earl of Huntington.

As early as the 1300s, references of Robin Hood appeared in written form. Ballads and poetry proclaimed Robin Hood's deeds. To this day stories and movies of Robin Hood's adventures are read and seen around the world.

Activity

Robin Hood is considered an English folk hero. Find out more about Robin Hood and his deeds. Then do some comparisons with American backwoods heroes such as Davy Crockett or Daniel Boone. Three books that might be helpful are *Robin Hood of Sherwood Forest* by Ann McGovern (Scholastic, 1968), *Davy Crockett* by Laurence Santry (Troll, 1983), and *Daniel Boone* by Laurie Lawlor (Whitman, 1988).

Use the Venn diagram below or create one of your own that would compare and contrast these folk heroes.

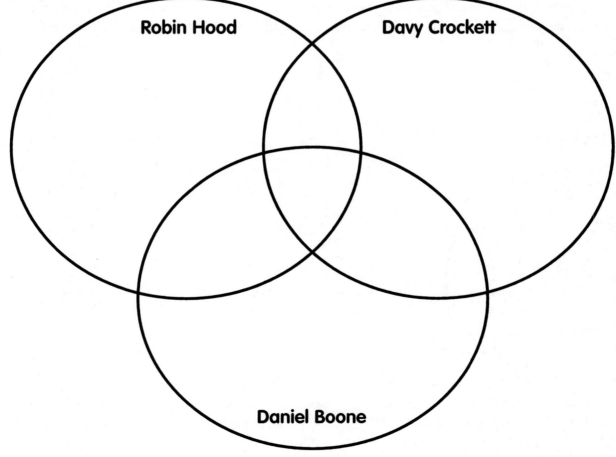

The Game of Golf

The game of golf as it is known today probably originated in Scotland. In 1744, the rules of this game were first written down. The Honourable Company of Edinburgh Golfers in Edinburgh, Scotland, is credited with this accomplishment. The rules governed play and helped quiet disturbances that may have been caused by the playing of the game.

The standard 18-hole golf game was established by the Royal and Ancient Golf Club of St. Andrews founded in 1754. Golf was particularly popular in Scotland and eventually spread throughout England and the rest of the British Commonwealth. It wasn't until 1829 that another golf club opened outside of Britain. This was the Royal Calcutta in India. In the 1700s golf may have been played in the United States, with many golf clubs founded in the 1880s. The rules used today internationally in golf are in cooperation of the United States Golf Association and the Great Britain and Royal and Ancient Golf Club of St. Andrews. These rules were originally established in 1951.

Golf is a popular sport today played throughout the world. There are professional men and women golfers. Many of these people play on the European tour based in Britain, the South African tour, the Australia/New Zealand tour, and the U.S. Professional Golf Association (PGA).

Activity

Near the end of each hole in golf there is a putting green. A special club called a putter is used to hit the ball into the hole. Set up a putting green in your classroom. For this you will need a putter, a few golf balls, a large carpet remnant, carpet squares or a small rug, a clean can or paper cup, and masking tape.

Set the carpet onto a cleared area. Set the can or cup onto its side. Mark an X on the carpet about six feet (180 cm) away from the can. Set the ball onto the X and gently "putt" it into the can. Count the number of strokes that it takes to get it into the can. As an extension, set up a putting tournament in your classroom, allowing everyone to take turns putting the ball.

London

In your trip around the world, you have been allotted one day to sightsee in London, England. London is the capital of the United Kingdom of Great Britain and Northern Ireland. As the ninth largest city in the world whose history goes back more than 2,000 years, London provides many sites to see and places to go. Before you begin your visit, do some planning. Look at the list of places below. Find out about each and write a brief description. Then decide which of these you want to visit.

London is filled with historic sights. You will be among about eight million tourists visiting London this year.

Use the map on page 114 to plan your tour beginning at Trafalgar Square. Mark your route in the order that you plan to visit the various sights.

Sights To See In London

Order of Visit	Sight	Description
	Trafalgar Square	
	Houses of Parliament	
	Piccadilly Circus	
	Victoria Station	
	Thames River	
	Buckingham Palace	
	Westminster Abbey	
	St. James Park	
	The British Museum	
	The National Gallery	
	Covent Garden	

Map of London

Using the map below, plan your day in London. Begin by taking a tour of the city on a double-decker bus to get a feel for the sights you might later visit.

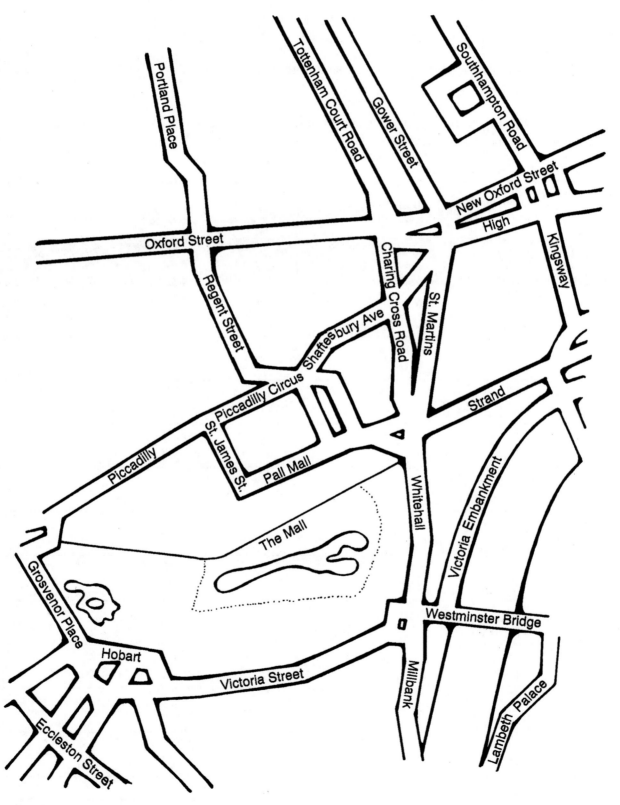

Norway

1. **Map of the Norway,** page 117

   Discuss the country's location, borders, geographical features, climate, and cities.

   Extending Activities:

   Assign group reports on the following topics:

   - Geographical diversity, ranging from the Trondheim Lowlands to the Southeastern Lowlands to the Mountains Plateau
   - Fjords
   - The Gulf Stream warming influence

2. **Facts About Norway; Norwegian Words and Phrases,** page 118

   Have students color the flag.

   Assign reports as suggested on page 4.

   Practice saying the Norwegian words and phrases.

   Ask students to use them in sentences. Note similarities to some English words.

3. **Day Names Research,** page 119

   Extending Activities:

   - Learn the names for the days of the week in Norwegian, in German, in Swedish, in Danish. Are they the same? Very similar?
   - Research the names for our months. From where do they come? What do they mean?

4. **The Skald,** page 120

   Extending Activities:

   - Collect alliterative poetry in class booklets.
   - Practice alliterative word play, tongue twisters, etc.
   - Convert a modern adventure hero story—eg., Superman, Batman, etc.,—into an alliterative adventure. Tell the story to others as if you were the skald who had been along with the hero and watched his daring deeds.

5. **Storytelling—Norse Gods and Giants,** page 120

   Extending Activities:

   - Assign individual reading of specific Norse myths.
   - Visualization: Make lists of characteristics of an individual mythic figure—i.e., Odin has one eye, a golden arm band, ravens perched on his shoulders, etc. Then have students draw and color the figure as they visualize him. Thor, Loki, Balder, Freya, and the trolls, giants, wolves, and serpents are all good subjects for this activity.
   - After reading about Odin's sending the warrior maidens to recover fallen heroes to Valhalla, listen to Wagner's Die Valkyrie.
   - Make puppets and reenact one of the Norse myths—one of Loki's escapades, for example. Construct stage, write dialogue, perform the play for other classes.

6. **Viking Museum,** page 121

   Extending Activities:

   - On an outline map of the world, have students trace Viking routes of trade, conquest, and exploration.
   - On a globe, have small groups locate specific sites of Viking colonization or trade. Place small colored, removeable stars at these points. Display wide range of coverage.
   - Research and write reports on explorations of Eric the Red and Leif Ericson.
   - Research origin of the word "berserk."
   - Make models of Viking helmets, battle-axes, spears, and swords.
   - Research, write, and give oral reports on burial customs of ancient Vikings.
   - Navigation—research Viking knowledge and use of astronomy for seafaring. Make charts and share with class.
   - Explain why the Viking Long Boat was ideally suited to raiding.
   - Report on the settlement of Iceland, its present language, culture, etc.

...Soaring solo, super...

Norway *(cont.)*

7. **Troll Treasure Trek,** pages 122-124

   Answers to Questions for Troll Treasure Trek

   1. 56 mi. (km)
   2. 60 mi. (km)
   3. 24 mi. (km)
   4. 60–24=36 mi. (km)
   5. 19 mi. (km)
   6. 56–19=37 mi. (km)
   7. 7 mi. (km)
   8. North
   9. 9 mi. (km)
   10. East
   11. 14 mi. (km)
   12. 17 mi. (km)
   13. Ingri. She traveled 4 mi. (km) farther in the same time.

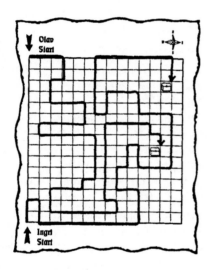

   Extending activities:

   • Discuss differences between alpine skiing and cross country skiing—types of skis, boots, nature of physical preparation, popularity as a sport, practicality, etc.
   • Prepare small group reports on survival in the far north environment—equipment, nutrition, techniques, preparation, clothing, navigation, health, etc.
   • Research and report on animals and birds of the north—reindeer, lemming, marten, wolf, artic fox, ermine, muskox, carribou, puffin, ptarmigan, snowy owl.
   • Research and report on Lappland and its inhabitants, language, culture, history, etc.
   • Research and report on Norway's use of military ski troops.

8. **Norwegian Food**

   Extending Activities:

   • Look at recipes from Norwegian cookbooks
   • Look at menus from local Scandinavian restaurants.
   • Prepare Scandinavian food favorites in class or at school if possible. Holiday foods are specialties and many times are available in season at bakeries.
   • Research the average calorie consumption in Norse countries as opposed to countries in more temperate climes. Discuss the reasons for any differences that might appear.
   • Examine research into relative consumption of fats, sugars, and carbohydrates in Norse lands. Discuss any differences that might exist in more temperate climates.

Bibliography

Fiction

Huygen, Will. *Gnomes.* (Abrams, 1977)

Magnus, Erica. *The Boy and the Devil.* (Carolrhoda Books, 1986)

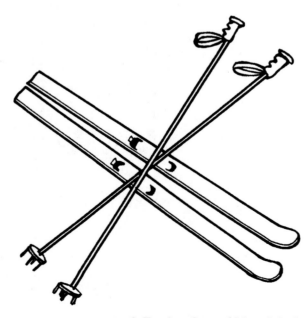

Map of Norway

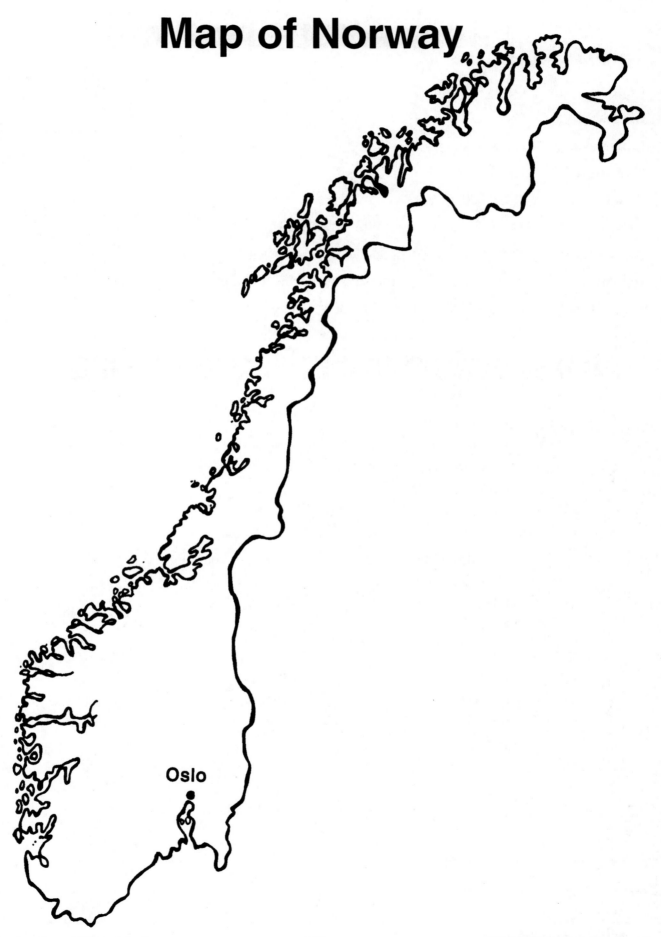

Oslo

Facts About Norway

Capital:	Oslo
Largest city:	Oslo
Language:	Norwegian
Currency:	Krone
Population:	4,420,000
Area:	149,405, 000 sq. mi. (386,958 sq. km)
Agriculture:	Barley, hay, livestock, potatoes, fruit, vegetables, timber
Industry:	Aluminum, fishing, forestry, chemicals, mining
Flag colors:	Cross—blue with white borders, Background—red

Norwegian Words and Phrases

God morgen	Good morning
God dag	Good day
God aften	Good evening
God natt	Good night
Hallo	Hello
Takk	Thank you
Hvordan star det til?	How are you?
Hva heter du?	What is your name?
Brod	Bread
Bror	Brother
Stol	Chair
Kaffe	Coffee
Fingeren	Finger
Fisk	Fish
Ja	Yes
Nei	No

Add three words or phrases that you want to learn in Norwegian.

_____

_____

_____

Day Names

When you arrive in Oslo, you are entering a land of the north. In fact, that is why the people of this area have been called Norsemen down through the ages. Norway, of course, has the same word root in its name. One-third of this nation lies above the Arctic Circle, and it borders in the east and north on Sweden, Finland, and Russia. Its western border is seacoast with hundreds of deep, long inlets called fjords. This makes the geography of Norway somewhat unusual. Because of its location, the far-northern portion of Norway has 24 hours of sunshine from mid-May through July. It is sometimes called the "land of the midnight sun."

The ancestors of the Norwegians were called Vikings. They were a daring, seafaring people who conducted fierce raids and adventurous voyages. For a period of about 300 years throughout northern Europe, in some cases reaching into the Mediterranean and even to the shores of North America, the Vikings roamed, traded, and raided.

Activity

One of the Norse cultural gifts to the world was a rich body of storytelling, saga, myth, and legend. Sometimes we are not even aware of how much such old beliefs and legends still influence our lives and culture. The names for the days of the week are a good example of this. Most of them are names referring to old gods or deities worshiped by ancient peoples. Complete the following chart by explaining the origin of the name for each day in the week. You may find information by looking up each name in encyclopedias or other reference books.

Days of the Week	The Story Behind the Names
Sunday	
Monday	
Tuesday	
Wednesday	
Thursday	
Friday	
Saturday	

Did you find that the majority of names were Norse?

Extension: Draw a picture of each figure represented by the weekday names.

Storytelling

The Skald

The favorite form of literature among the early Norse people was poetry. They told great stories of battle and adventure. In fact, Viking warriors would often make sure they had a skald—a poet-storyteller—along with them whenever they went into battle. Highly respected for his skill in using words, the skald would compose a story of their voyage and tell it to the assembled company upon returning from their dangerous quests. Instead of rhyming the word endings, the skald used a technique called "alliteration." This meant beginning several words in each line with the same sound. Here is an example:

> "The Spear-raiders sailed long over the lonely seas,
>
> Ever failing to find friends, only eager enemies."

Did you hear the "ess" and "ell" sounds repeated in the first line? What sounds were repeated in the second line?

Write your own Norse saga, telling a tale of adventure—warriors sailing to a far shore, battling enemies, perhaps slaying a dragon, and returning home. See if you can use alliteration two to three times in each line. Underline the parts of the words that are alliterative in each line.

Norse Mythology

Like the traditional myths of many cultures, the Norse stories come to us across the mists of time as oral tales passed down from generation to generation. This is still one of the best ways to enjoy these ancient stories. Read freely to the class from *D'Aulaire's Norse Gods and Giants.* (See Bibliography.) Following are some recommended selections: "Introduction"; "The First Gods and Giants"; "The Creation of the World,"; "The Creation of Man"; Yggdrasil, the World Tree"; "Asgard and the Aesir Gods";

"Odin, the All-father"; "Thor, the Thunder-god"; "Thor and the Jotun Utgardsloki."

Viking Museum

When you visit a Viking museum in Oslo, you will see actual relics and representations of old Norse craftsmanship. The old Vikings' lives were dependent upon their boats and their weapons, so they rightfully admired good design, practicality, usefulness, hardiness, and beauty. They made spears, battle-axes, shields, and beautiful "long boats" with graceful dragon or serpent heads carved on the curved prows. The boats could hold 15 to 30 pairs of oars. When the wind blew, they would hoist a large rectangular sail to pull them swiftly over the billows. Otherwise, the warriors would place their shields along the boat side and man the oars. The boats had keels to keep them from rolling too much and to permit easier steering. They were sturdy, made of oak planks, yet fast and easy to pull ashore ideal vessels for lightning raids on unsuspecting farms and villages. The boats ranged from about 65 feet (20 m) to 95 feet (30 m) long. Examine the picture below and build a Viking long boat from modeling clay.

Materials:

modeling clay	tagboard for shields
colored markers	new pencils or dowels to use as masts
straight pins	white construction paper for sails
craftsticks for oars	cardboard for stern and prow extensions

Directions: Model the hull of the boat similar to a canoe shape. Draw serpent/dragon head patterns on cardboard and cut out. Attach the heads to the prow of the boat. Cut out small circles of tagboard to represent shields. Decorate and attach to gunwales of boat with straight pin. Slip craft sticks between shields to represent oars.

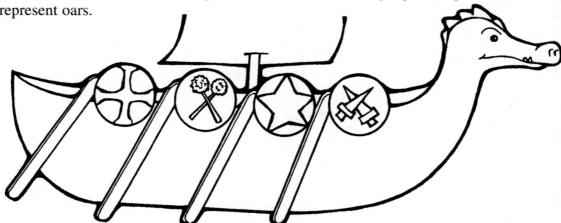

Place mast in center of boat, pushing base through clay bottom to form support. Cut rectangular sail from construction paper, decorate with dragon or geometric design. At the midpoint of each long side, punch holes near the edge of the sail. Thread the sail on the mast, using both holes and letting the tension hold the bend as if it were in a stiff gale.

Extensions:

- Define and use in sentences the terms: prow, stern, gunwale, keel, and mast.
- On an outline map of the world, trace Viking routes of exploration and conquest.
- On a classroom globe, have small groups locate specific points of Viking seafaring destinations. Then place small removable colored stars at these sites—for example, Iceland, Greenland, Dublin, the Black Sea, etc.

Troll Treasure Trek

Ingri and Olav, like many other Norwegians, were very good cross country skiers and loved to go on long treks through the snowy forests and mountains. The two cousins knew all of the ancient Norse stories of the trolls and frost-giants of Jotunheim and the gold and gems these creatures had stolen from the gnomes of Darkalfheim. One two-headed troll—Doppelkopf was his name—hid his treasure in two places because his two heads could not agree on one hiding place. The two cousins decided to try to find the treasure. They each set out from their homes one day, following directions from the clues in the ancient stories they had learned so well. Following are the directions (N=north, S=south, E=east, W=west) and the distances (in miles or kilometers) each one traveled.

Olav

1. E-3
2. S-2
3. W-1
4. S-2
5. E-3
6. S-2
7. W-4
8. S-1
9. E-5
10. S-4
11. W-1
12. S-1
13. W-3
14. S-2
15. E-6
16. N-1
17. W-1
18. N-7
19. E-4
20. S-1
21. E-1
22. S-1 (Treasure!)

Ingri

1. N-2
2. E-1
3. S-2
4. E-9
5. N-3
6. W-2
7. N-2
8. E-1
9. N-2
10. E-1
11. S-2
12. E-3
13. N-5
14. W-3
15. N-2
16. W-3
17. S-2
18. W-1
19. N-5
20. E-7
21. S-2 (Treasure!)

Troll Treasure Trek *(cont.)*

On the grid map on the next page, use red pencil to trace the path for Olav and blue for Ingri. The sides for all the squares on the grid are exactly one mile (or one kilometer) in length. When you have finished and have traced each path to its destination, answer the following questions.

1. How many miles (kilometers) did Olav ski? _____

2. How many miles (kilometers) did Ingri ski? _____

3. If Ingri had been able to ski the shortest distance in a straight line east and then north, how many miles (kilometers) would she have skied?

   _____

4. By following the clues from the Norse myths, how many extra miles (kilometers) did she have to ski?

   _____

5. If Olav had been able to ski the shortest distance in a straight line east and then south, how many miles (kilometers) would he have skied?

   _____

6. By following the clues from the Norse myths, how many extra miles (kilometers) did he have to ski?

   _____

7. What was the longest distance Olav skied in one direction? _____

8. What direction was he traveling then? _____

9. What was the longest distance Ingri skied in one direction? _____

10. What direction was she traveling then? _____

11. If Ingri took her treasure directly west and north to Olav's house, what is the shortest distance she would have to ski?

   _____

12. If Olav took his treasure directly south and west to Ingri's house, what is the shortest distance he would have to ski?

   _____

13. If both Ingri and Olav left home at the same time and arrived at the treasure troves at the same time, who do you think was the faster skier? Why?

   _____

Extension: When all Troll Treasure Treks are finished, have students draw their most vivid renditions of the two-headed troll, Doppelkopf. Color them and attach their treasure trek maps to the bottom. Display.

Troll Treasure Trek Grid Map

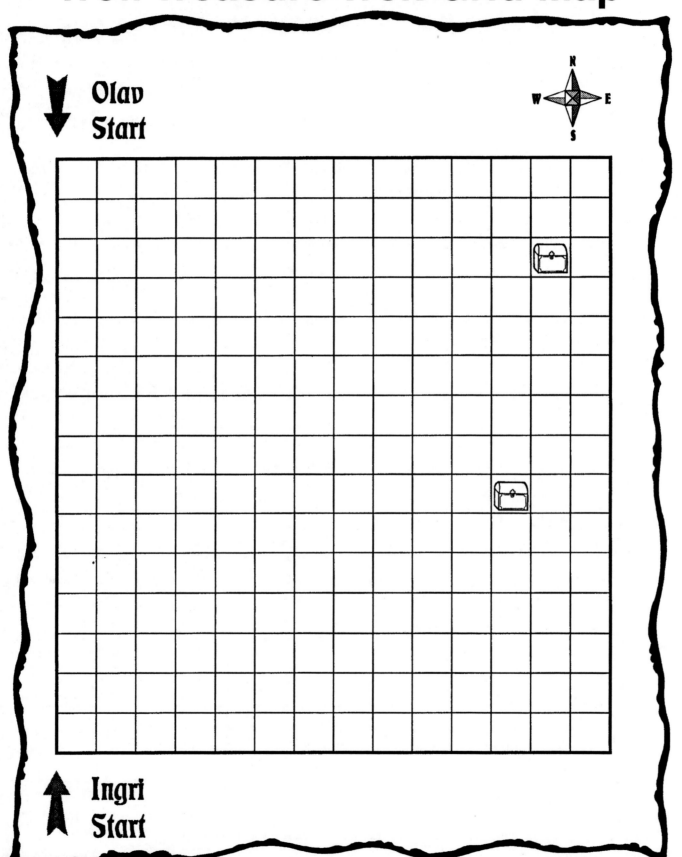

Egypt

1. **Map of Egypt,** page 126

   Discuss the country's location, borders, geographical features, climate and cities.

   Extending Activities:

   Assign group reports on the following topics:

   • Geographical diversity, ranging from fertile Nile valley to arid, forbidding desert

   • Search for the source of the Nile

   • Importance of the Delta

   • Boat construction for river traffic

2. **Facts About Egypt; Arabic Words and Phrases,** page 127

   Have students color the flag.

   Assign reports as suggested on page 4.

   Practice saying the Arabic words and phrases. Ask students to use them in sentences.

3. **Ancient Egypt,** page 128

   Extending Activities:

   • Find out more about ancient Egypt vs. modern Egypt.

   • Discuss the changes that have altered Egypt, politically, geographically, and economically.

   • Notice the changes in western and eastern boundaries.

   • Research the Suez Canal.

   • Research ancient Alexandria, importance of its library.

4. **Water and Paper,** page 129

   Extending Activities:

   Prepare reports on following:

   Papyrus making; early libraries; irrigation methods of old; problems of flooding.

5. **Hieroglyphics,** page 130

   Extending Activities:

   Small group projects/reports on the following topics:

   • Discoverer of the Rosetta Stone

   • Deciphering of the Code

   • Writing—its importance to the Egyptians

   • Invention of the Alphabet

   • Egyptian number system

   • Make your own Rosetta Stone using clay, writing hieroglyphics with a toothpick.

   • Make a cartouche (name tag) which hangs from neck.

   Make your own clay using 2 cups (500 mL) flour, 1 cup (250 mL) salt, 2 Tbs. (15 mL) mineral oil, and 2 cups (500 mL) boiling water.

Shape clay into flat ovals, make a hole for hanging on one end. When dry, paint with gold or black paint, dry and scratch hieroglyphics to show your name.

6. **Animals of the Nile,** page 131

   Extending Activities:

   • Find out which ancient Egyptian gods were represented by the following animals: cats, hippos, cows, jackals, crocodiles.

   • Construct a chart showing each of the above animals and the gods represented. Tell why the hippo was hunted and which animals were mummified and why.

   • Report on oxen and their use.

   • Compare jackals, dingoes, and coyotes: bring in pictures, show habitat, describe behavior.

   • Prepare reports on camels: size, average length of life, adaptation to desert environment, racing speed, disposition, ease of training, comfort for the rider, etc.

   • Prepare mural of animals of Egypt, showing pictures and characteristics of each against a background map of Egypt.

7. **Pyramids,** page 132

   Extending Activities:

   • Assign small groups to research, prepare charts or models for, and explain the construction of the following structures: The Great Pyramid of King Khufu, The Great Sphinx, The tomb of King Tutankhamen (King Tut).

   • Assign reports on ancient Egyptian religious beliefs and the importance of these major deities: Amon-Re, Re, Osiris, Isis.

8. **Adventure,** page 133

   • Read about the search for the Nile headwaters.

   • Read about Stanley and Livingstone.

   • Bring in pictures of the treasures of King Tut's tomb.

   • Show slides, film, or videos of Egyptian art and recurring motifs of cats, scarabs, stylized figures of humans and animals.

Bibliography

Nonfiction

Aliki. *Mummies Made in Egypt.* (Harper Trophy, 1979)

Gibling, James Cross. *The Riddle of the Rosetta Stone; Key to Ancient Egypt.* (HarperCollins, 1990)

Hart, George. *Eyewitness: Ancient Egypt.* (Library Binding, 2000)

Fiction

Climo, Shirley. *The Egyptian Cinderella.* (Harper, 1989)

Green, Roger. *Tales of Ancient Egypt.* (Penguin, 1972)

Snyder, Zilpha Keatley. *The Egypt Game.* (Dell, 1967)

Map of Egypt

Cairo

Facts About Egypt

Capital:	Cairo
Largest city:	Cairo
Language:	Arabic
Currency:	Egyptian pound
Population:	69,536,000
Area:	386,662 sq. mi. (1,001,449 sq. km.)
Agriculture:	Cotton, corn, oranges, wheat
Industry:	Chemicals, cottons, fertilizer
Flag colors:	Top—red, Center—white, Bottom—black

Egyptian Words and Phrases

(The language spoken by most Egyptians today is Arabic.)

Es salaem alekum (Peace be upon you.)	Hello
Wa alekum es salaem (in response to above)	Hello to you
Kitaeb (kutub)	Books
Walad	Boy
Eysh (or Khubz)	Bread
Akh	Brother
Sayyara	Car
Kursi	Chair
Gibna	Cheese
Firaekh	Chicken
El medina	City
Eyn (or Inen)	Eyes
Ahwa	Coffee
Ab	Father
Qadam	Foot
Sabryi	Girl
Aywa (or Nalam)	Yes

List three other words or phrases you would like to learn in Arabic.

_____

_____

_____

Ancient Egypt

The map below shows an outline of ancient Egypt. Learn more about this country by labeling the map with the following: Western Desert, Eastern Desert, the ancient cities of Karnak and Thebes, Delta, Mediterranean Sea, Nile River, Red Sea, Lower Egypt, Upper Egypt. Color all bodies of water blue, the farmland green, and the deserts tan. Compare a current map of Egypt and list any changes you notice on the back of this paper.

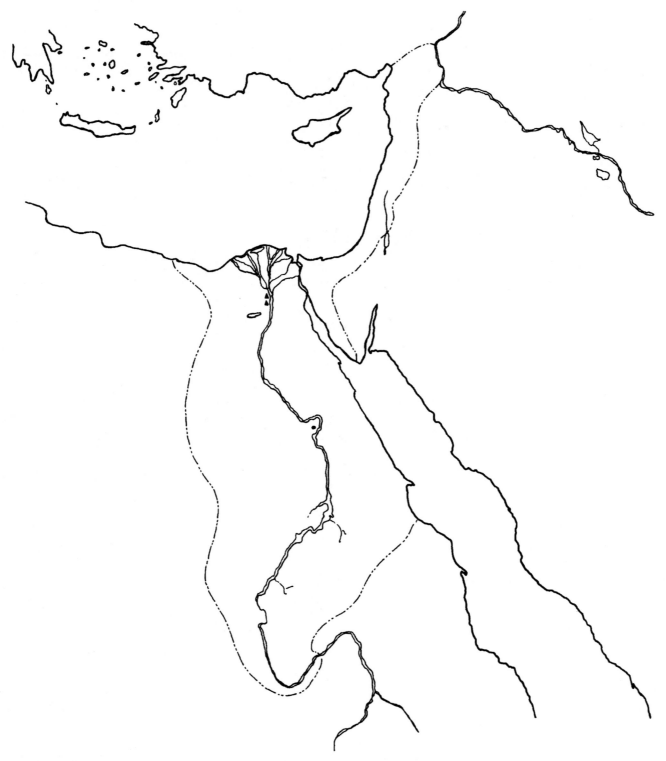

Water and Paper

Shaduf

Ancient Egyptians became skillful in agriculture. The banks of the Nile River were rich because of the fresh topsoil the river deposited in its yearly flooding. In order to water their crops regularly in this dry country, however, the people had to move water out of the river and into irrigation ditches. How did they do this? They invented a simple but ingenious device called a shaduf. Make your own shaduf using the directions and sketch below as a guide. Experiment with adding or subtracting stones in the bag to control the weight. Experiment with changing the length of the stick on each side of the balance point. (In science, this sort of machine is called a lever and fulcrum.) Notice that you can tip the bucket to pick up water from one place, raise it, turn it, and then lower it to deposit the water somewhere else.

Materials:
A strong forked branch from tree trimmings, 3 feet (1 m) long
A strong straight pole for the pail and bag, 3 feet (1 m) long
A small plastic or metal pail, 1 gallon (4 L)
A small plastic bag or basket to hang on the stick opposite the pail
Three short cords, 18 inches (45 cm) each, one to tie over the fork, and the others to fasten the pail and basket to the pole

Make your own papyrus.

After you have read how ancient Egyptians invented an early type of paper from papyrus (a reed growing on the river bank), try this activity to prepare for writing your own hieroglyphics.

Materials: tissue paper, large bowl of water, glue, sand screen sifter

Directions:

A. Tear up a bunch of tissue paper.

B. Put tissues in bowl of water with some glue added.

C. Put a handful of soaked tissues on the screen and press flat.

D. Lay piece of pressed tissue on paper towels to dry.

E. Using the information on page 130, paint your name in hieroglyphics on the papyrus after it has dried.

Hieroglyphics

We know much about ancient Egyptians because they left written records. Following Roman rule, however, people lost the ability to use hieroglyphics. Nobody was able to read these puzzling symbols for over 1,000 years. Finally in 1799, outside the city of Rosetta, Egypt, a large flat stone was found with both Greek and Egyptian symbols on it. Since the Greek symbols could be read, they were used to unlock the mystery. Using your own "Rosetta Stone" of hieroglyphics shown below, translate the passage. Then see if you can write your own hieroglyphic note on the back of the page.

Translate the passage using the clues given on your Rosetta Stone. Write the words on the lines provided. Some words are pictured phonetically, so letters may be missing.

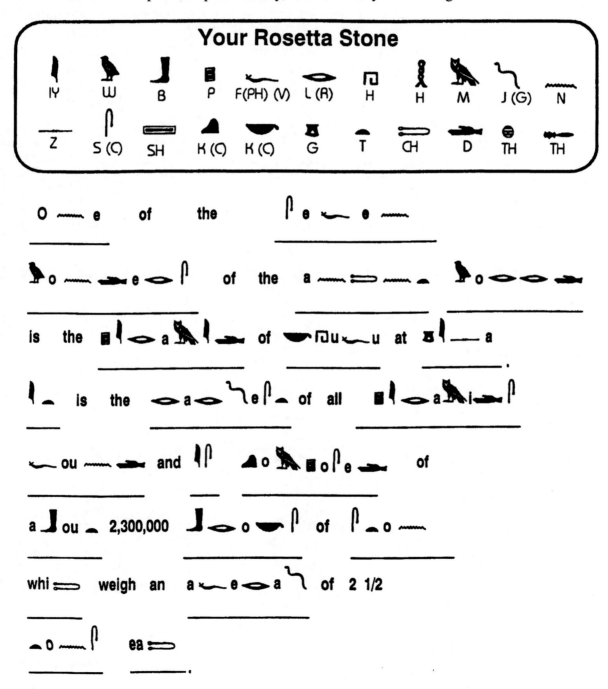

Animals of the Nile

Many different types of animals flourished in ancient Egypt. All kinds of birds made homes in the papyrus thickets beside the Nile. Nests of cormorants, geese, pintail ducks, and pelicans could be found there. In the river were catfish and perch. Along the banks one could find hippos and crocodiles sunning and playing in the water. Cats were everywhere, sometimes living in Egyptian homes. In the deserts, east and west of the river valley, one might see hyenas, jackals, rams, and oxen. Antelopes, gazelles, wild bulls, and lions were plentiful there.

In the wordsearch puzzle below, find and circle the animal names that appear in the paragraph above.

Research: See if you can locate ten facts about camels and/or cobras living in Egypt today. List these on the back of this paper.

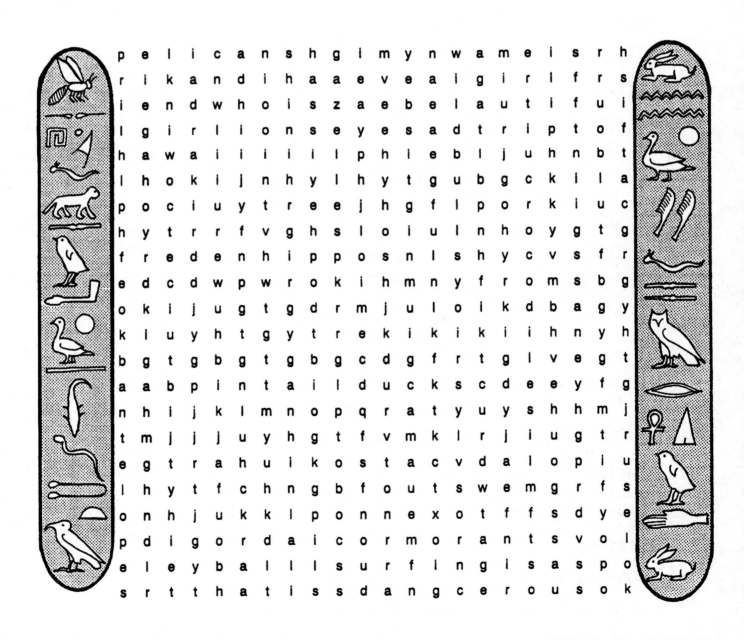

Pyramids

Known everywhere as one of the Seven Wonders of the Ancient World, the tombs for the kings of Egypt were pyramids—giant structures that required many years and thousands of laborers to construct. They also required a knowledge of mathematics and engineering, for the stones were very large, and the problems of moving and lifting such immense weights were many.

Build paper pyramids using the pattern and directions below. (The pattern may be enlarged with an overhead projector or copy machine.)

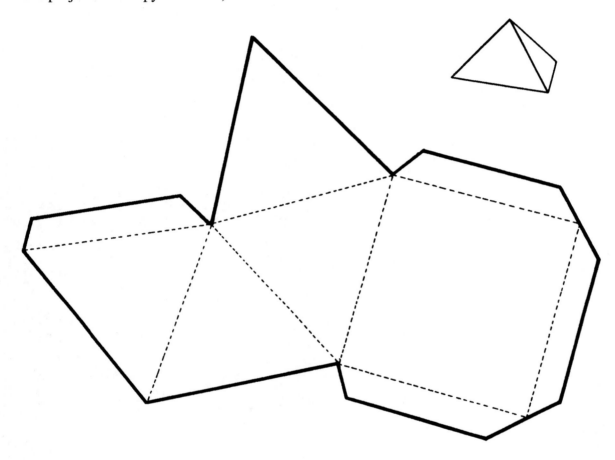

Directions: Cut the pattern along the solid lines. Fold tabs inward along all dashed lines. Glue or tape the tabs so that they remain inside the pyramid.

Activities: Before gluing or taping the tabs, do one or more of the following activities:

1. Measure the sides of the base. What pattern do you see? (The sides are equal in length.) What geometric figure is it? (square) Measure the triangles. Is one larger than the others? (No; they are all the same.) How far is it completely around the base? Can you figure out a way to measure the height of the pyramid? (Remember, the sides slope inward, so the pyramid is not as high as the length of a triangle side.)

2. Draw a message in hieroglyphics on each triangular side.

3. Compose a four-line poem. Write a separate line on each triangular side.

Adventure

You are an early adventurer exploring the wonders of an ancient land that contains exotic animals (cobras, hyenas, crocodiles), mysterious hidden tombs and mummies, treasures (gold, precious jewels, manuscripts). Write your story as you would tell it when you return after close escapes from death. Give your story a title and illustrate your cover page with something symbolic. If you wish, you may use the following beginning paragraph to get started.

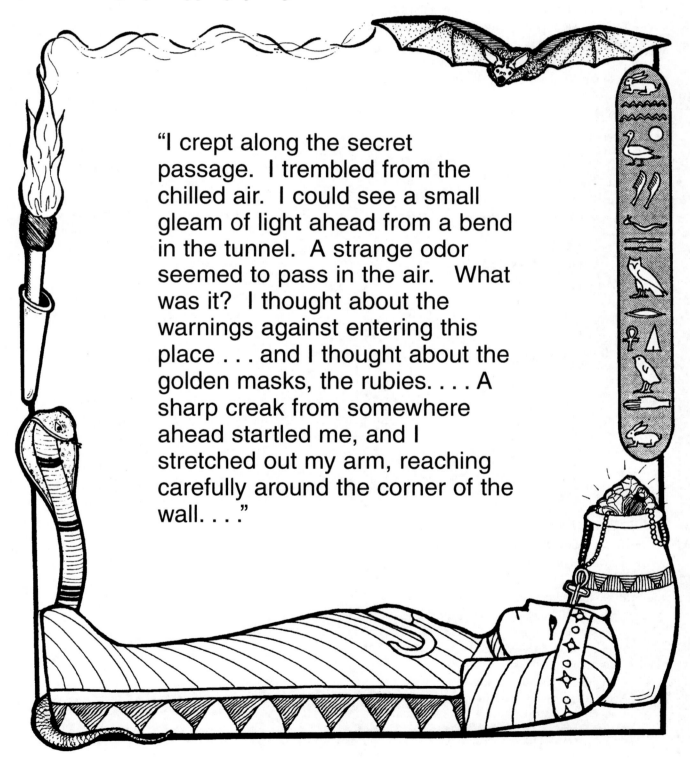

"I crept along the secret passage. I trembled from the chilled air. I could see a small gleam of light ahead from a bend in the tunnel. A strange odor seemed to pass in the air. What was it? I thought about the warnings against entering this place . . . and I thought about the golden masks, the rubies. . . . A sharp creak from somewhere ahead startled me, and I stretched out my arm, reaching carefully around the corner of the wall. . . ."

Kenya

1. **Map of Kenya,** page 136

   Discuss the country's location, borders, geographical features, climate, and cities.

   Extending Activities:

   Assign group reports on the following topics:

   - Geographical diversity, ranging from tropical coastal area to dry plains to fertile highlands
   - Major Lakes—Lake Victoria, Lake Turkana, Lake Rudolph
   - Location on the equator—climate conditions

2. **Facts about Kenya; Swahili Words and Phrases,** page 137

   Have students color the flag.

   Assign reports as suggested on page 4.

   Practice saying the Swahili words and phrases. Ask students to use them in sentences.

3. **African Animal Safari**, page 138

   Answers to African Animal Safari

   1. . . . JACK ALways eats . . .
   2. . . . broccoLI ON the . . .
   3. . . . LoOK A PEncil is . . .
   4. . . . flopPY THONgs all . . .
   5. . . . tropHY ENAmel began . . .
   6. . . . FlAMING Over the . . .
   7. . . . hOST RICHly praised . . .
   8. . . . a daZE, BRAins…
   9. . . . MarCI VEToed every . . .
   10. . . . the mANTEL OPEn the . . .
   11. . . . amBUSH BABY giraffes . . .
   12. . . . A GOR, FIL Always . . .

   Extending Activities:

   - Take a field trip to nearest animal park or zoo.
   - View National Geographic videos of African wildlife.
   - Bring in pictures of all the animals listed.
   - Discuss wildlife ecology, endangered species, and extinction.
   - Prepare an endangered species chart with accompanying pictures.
   - Develop class consensus for African Animal Yearbook, containing cut out pictures of "Most Dangerous," "Most Unusual," "Most Beautiful," "Most Majestic," "Largest," "Smallest," "Fastest," "Most colorful," etc.

4. **Moja To Kumi,** pages 139-140

   Answers to problems 1-10.

   1 = Mbili (20
   2 = Saba (7)
   3 = Tisa (9)
   4 = Tano (5)
   5 = Kumi (10)
   6 = Tisa (9)
   7 = Mbili (2)
   8 = Kumi (10)
   9 = Tatu (3)
   10 = Mbili (2)

   Extending Activities:

   - Learn Swahili numbers for teens. Simply add numbers to ten with the particle na—for example, eleven is kumi na moja (10 plus 1), twelve is kumi na mbili, thirteen is kumi na tatu, etc. Ishirini is the word for twenty.
   - Number objects and manipulatives in the classroom with Swahili number names.
   - Practice oral number facts under ten in Swahili.
   - Develop simple addition or counting games with facts up to twenty.

5. **Kenya Geography—Relief Map,** page 141

   Extending Activities:

   - Examine a relief globe. Note how rivers drain the land of run-off from the highlands and mountains.
   - Trace the path of the Nile from headwaters north through Cairo to the Mediterranean sea.
   - Examine how climate changes as elevation increases. (Mt. Kenya and Mt. Kilimanjaro are very close to the equator, yet may be snowcapped.)

Kenya *(cont.)*

6. **Kenya Humidity — Hygrometer,** page 142

Extending Activities:

- Compare relative humidity figures for different parts of the world—for example, Antartica and Cuba, Hawaii and Australian outback, Calcutta and Los Angeles, etc.
- Develop a comfort chart, showing places with similar temperatures during the summer but widely differing relative humidity figures.
- Discuss sauna baths and their effects on the body. How are they different from simple high temperatures?
- Discuss why keeping records of such figures is of benefit to scientists and others.

7. **Storytelling**

Extending Activities:

- In small groups, write a puppet play for one of the African myths or the students' original stories. (See bibliography.)
- Make the puppets, the stage, and present a production as a class or small group project.
- Illustrate your collection of New African Fables.
- With a narrator guiding the story, present a pantomime of one of the stories, using as many characters as are needed. Masks may be designed to represent animals and other characters.

8. **African Jewelry—Beads,** page 143

Extending Activities:

- Tie dye old T-shirts to make African shirts.
- Make natural dyes for the following colors: yellow, dandelion blossoms; brown, coffee; purple, grape juice; red, beets; green, spinach leaves.

  Materials and Directions for Making Natural Dyes:

  > 1 quart (1 L) water
  > 8 ounces (300 mL) plant material
  > 1 Tbs. (15 mL) salt
  > 1 Tbs. (15 mL) white vinegar

Mix and simmer one hour, soak overnight for stronger color, strain.

9. **African Masks,** page 144

Extending Activities:

- Make African huts from construction paper bent into rounds. Stand on edge and use dried grass to cover conical construction paper roof.

- Make African shields using large pieces of cardboard from cartons and spears using long cardboard tubes for spears. Decorate oval-shaped shields with designs similar to the masks, using bold colors, raffia, etc. Spear heads may also have small bundles of dried grass or raffia attached.

10. **Make a Corn-Based Stew**

- Kenyans use corn (called maize) as a basic food to which they add other ingredients. Corn is ground into a kind of porridge. Vegetables are added (and sometimes meat or fish) to make a stew. Make a porridge from cornmeal. Enjoy the taste of food made from corn. Prepare creamed corn (adding other vegetables if desired) or corn chowder.

Bibliography

Fiction

Brown, Marcia. *Shadow.* (Macmillan Child Group, 1986)

Courlander, Harold. *The Cow-Tail Switch & Other African Stories.* (Henry Holt & Co., 1987)

Dayrell, Elpinston. *Why the Sun and Moon Live in the Sky.* (Houghton Mifflin, 1990)

Kipling, Rudyard. *The Elephant's Child.* (Dutton Child Books, 1992)

Kipling, Rudyard. *How the Rhinoceros Got His Skin.* (Picture Book Studio, 1991)

Winther, Barbara. *Plays from African Tales.* (Plays, 1992)

Cole, Joanna. *Best Loved Folktales of the World.* (Anchor Books, Doubleday 1983)

Visuals

Africa (a multicultural set of 18 posters with text on history, culture, religion, & art forms)

Write to:
Art Visuals
Visual Aids for Visual Arts
P.O. Box 925
Orem, UT 84059-0925

Map of Kenya

● **Nairobi**

Facts About Kenya

Capital:	Nairobi
Largest city:	Nairobi
Language:	Swahili
Currency:	Shilling
Population:	30,766,000
Area:	224,081 sq. mi. (580,367 sq. km)
Agriculture:	Bananas, beef cattle, cassava, coffee, sisal, wheat
Industry:	Cement, chemicals, textiles, light machinery
Flag colors:	Top—black, Center—red-orange, Bottom—green, Shield—red-orange with crossed white spears (Sections are separated by narrow white bars.)

Kenyan Words and Phrases

(Swahili is a language spoken by most Kenyans. It is called the national language. English is called the official language.)

Jambo	Hello
Habari Yako?	How are you?
Jina lako nani?	What is your name?
Ndiyo	Yes
La	No
Kijana	Boy
Msichana	Girl
Baba	Father
Mama	Mother
Mkate	Bread
Motakari	Car
Pesa	Money
Shule	School
Viatu	Shoes
Maji	Water
Safari	Journey

Add three words or phrases that you want to learn in Swahili.

_____

_____

_____

Visit a Wild Game Park

Now that you have arrived in Nairobi from Egypt, you will want to visit a wild game park, for here in Kenya are found some of the most varied and spectacular animals of the world. Among them are the following mammals, reptiles, and birds.

aardvark	aardwolf	antelope
baboon	water buffalo	bush baby
cheetah	chimpanzee	civet
wild dogs	elephant	gazelle
genet	gerenuk	giraffe
gorilla	hippopotamus	warthog
hyena	hydrax	impala
jackal	leopard	lion
okape	rhinoceros	wildebeest
zebra	crocodile	python
vulture	ostrich	flamingo

Shaduf

Many of these animals possess protective coloring that allows them to remain hidden in their native habitat. In somewhat the same way, animal names remain hidden in the following sentences. If you are good hunters, you may be able to spot some of them. Underline the names of as many as you can. The first one has been located to give you a start.

1. I notice that <u>Jack</u> always eats his spinach.
2. Shirley, however, always leaves her broccoli on the plate.
3. Stefan the clown said, "Look, a pencil is balanced on my nose."
4. "I don't know why she wore those floppy thongs to our party!
5. As the years passed, the trophy enamel began to peel away.
6. When the chef turned away, the steaks began flaming over the glowing coals.
7. Our host richly praised the guests colorful costumes.
8. The injured man was in a daze, brains jarred by the crash on the highway.
9. As class president, Marci vetoed every proposal we made.
10. Take the clock from the mantel, open the face, and wind it up.
11. Poachers often try to ambush baby giraffes for profit.
12. "Igor, I'll always remember you," said Dr. Frankenstein.

Now, see if you can hide the names of any two animals in two original sentences of your own.

13. _____

14. _____

Mojo to Kumi

Jambo, world travelers! After counting how many African animals you were able to locate (even when they were hidden) you might like to learn to count in Swahili. Following are the Swahili numbers from one to ten:

One	Moja (MOH-jah)		**Six**	Sita (SEE-tah)
Two	Mbili (MBEE-lee)		**Seven**	Saba (SAH-bah)
Three	Tatu (TAH-too)		**Eight**	Nane (NAH-neh)
Four	Nne (N-neh)		**Nine**	Tisa (TEE-sah)
Five	Tano (TAH-noh)		**Ten**	Kumi (KOO-mee)

Most of these should be easy for you to pronounce. (The numbers two and four may take a bit of extra practice.)

Activity

1. As a whole class, practice counting from one to ten in unison. Do this until the sound is fairly well ingrained and uniform.

2. Then in groups of two to four, practice memorizing the numbers in order.

3. Finally, practice reading in random order the sentences from the African Animal Safari (one to ten only). With their Safari Sentences in front of them, ask students to identify in Swahili which sentence number you have read.

4. A perfect score, of course, is KUMI!

Mojo to Kumi *(cont.)*

Answer the following questions with Swahili numbers only.

1.
Kumi – nane =

2.
Mbili + tano =

3.
Tatu + sita =

4.
Moja + nne =

5.
Mbili x tano =

6.
Tatu x tatu =

7.
Tisa – saba =

8.
Kumi x moja =

9.
Sita ÷ mbili =

10.
Nane ÷ nne =

Again, a perfect score is KUMI!

Relief Map

Kenya is located right on the earth's equator and features some of the planet's most interesting geography. The country may be divided into three main sections: the tropical coastal area, the generally dry plains area, and the fertile highlands. Just across its southern border you may see Mt. Kilimanjaro, Africa's tallest peak. Within the borders lie Mt Kenya, second highest mountain on the continent, Lake Turkana, and part of Lake Victoria, the second largest fresh water lake in the world. Running north and south through the country is one of the world's most interesting features. It contains some of Kenya's most fertile ground, and some of the world's singular anthropological finds. Find the name of this unique African geological feature in the following activity.

Materials: plaster of Paris (available at craft stores), poster paint, white poster board

Directions:

A. In small groups, draw outline maps of Kenya on white poster board.

B. Sketch the following features inside the outlines:

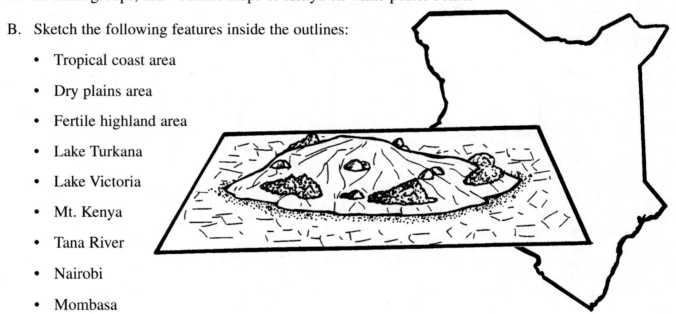

- Tropical coast area

- Dry plains area

- Fertile highland area

- Lake Turkana

- Lake Victoria

- Mt. Kenya

- Tana River

- Nairobi

- Mombasa

C. After these features have been sketched, mix your plaster of Paris and build up the land, remembering to put in depressions for the lakes, valleys, rivers, and lowlands.

D. Allow to dry.

E. Paint water areas blue, fertile areas green, dry plains areas tan.

F. With small neatly printed tags, label all features listed in B above.

G. Lastly, ink a faint dark line across the proper part of your relief maps to represent the equator. Label it.

Kenya Hygrometer

As we know, most of Africa is hot. In fact, the earth's highest temperature was recorded in Libya in 1922—136° Fahrenheit (57.7° Celsius). The earth's highest annual mean temperature was recorded between 1960 and 1966 in Ethiopia, just north of Kenya. It was 94° Fahrenheit (34.4° Celsius). Now that you have made your relief maps, you will know that Mombasa is on the coast in a humid area. Humidity is the amount of moisture in the air. We feel much more discomfort when the moisture in the air is high, especially when the temperature is high also. Scientists can tell how much moisture the air can absorb and how much it actually has absorbed. That figure is called "relative humidity." The instrument they use to record this information is called a "hygrometer." You can build your own hygrometer very easily by following these directions.

Materials:
2 room thermometers
small piece of cotton material
(*Large, old tubular shoelaces*
work well sometimes.)
a quart milk carton
scissors
rubber bands
thread

Directions:

1. Make sure the thermometers read the same temperature.

2. Cover the bulb of one thermometer with a 3-inch (8cm) scrap of cotton or shoestring. Tie it with thread, leaving a tail to hang down as shown.

3. Use rubber bands to attach the two thermometers to adjacent sides of the milk carton as shown.

4. Poke a small hole in the carton just below the bulb of the thermometer with the tail.

5. Push the tail through the hole.

6. Fill the carton with water up to the hole level. That will keep the thermometer tail (or wick) wet.

7. After an hour, read the two thermometers.

Results: You should get a lower reading on the "tail thermometer."

Explanation: Water evaporates from the moist wick and uses up heat, so the temperature drops on that thermometer. As long as the air can keep on absorbing the moisture, the thermometers will register different temperatures. The minute the air is filled with moisture, we will have 100% humidity, and the thermometers will show exactly the same temperature.

African Jewelry

Men and women throughout Africa love jewelry and wear it for appearance and for social purposes. Bracelets, earrings, necklaces, anklets, good luck charms—all are seen in colorful and inventive combinations, especially in beaded form. Share this African delight in ornament by making your own jewelry of your own design.

Materials:
various items that can be used for beads (buttons, shells, sequins, old beads, broken strings of beads, etc.)
dry macaroni, about 3 pounds (500 g) assorted sizes per class
string, yam, picture wire
clear tape
curtain rings, 1½ in. (4 cm) diameter
resealable sandwich bags
food coloring
rubbing alcohol

Procedure:

- Color macaroni for beads. Pour ½ tsp. (2.5 mL) of rubbing alcohol into a plastic sandwich bag to help the macaroni dry quickly. Add a few drops of coloring, depending on how deep you want the color to be. Then add macaroni, seal the bag and shake until dry. You may need to spread the macaroni on a paper towel if it does not dry completely in the bag.

- Bracelets and necklaces: Cut strings to desired lengths. Then thread beads, buttons, sequins, and macaroni on the strings in alternating shapes and colors according to your like. Knot one end of the string and tape the other to make the threading process easier. Tie off when completed.

- Earrings: Twist picture wire to form an oval, circle, or triangle with one long end. String beads on the wire in any design order you wish. Twist the wire together at the top and make a sizeable loop to hang over the ear according to the diagram below.

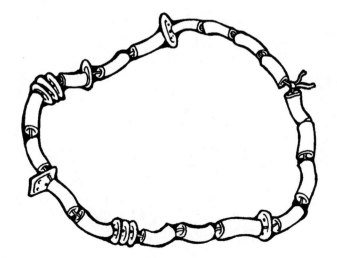

- Rings and ankle bracelets: Use variations of the above techniques.

African Masks

African societies have many social rituals, dances, and celebrations where they wear not only their colorful jewelry but also artistically designed and carved masks. These usually feature stylized geometric designs. It is fun to create your own inventive African masks to commemorate your visit to Kenya.

Materials:
large paper plates
construction paper—12" x 18" (30 cm x 45 cm) in brown, black, tan, and white
yarn, string, buttons, beads, fabric scraps, raffia, shells, seeds
scissors
glue

Procedure:

A. Use paper plate or construction paper as base for mask.

B. Draw a large outline of a face.

C. Glue geometric shapes to the front of the mask, layering smaller shapes on top. Make large facial features and cut out eye slits.

D. At the four corners of the mask, cut 1" to 2" (2.5 cm to 5 cm.) slits. Overlap the slits and staple or glue. This will pull the outside edges inward, giving the mask a shape to fit over the face.

E. Add bits of yarn, string, buttons, raffia, etc., to decorate the final mask.

F. Display masks on wall.